THE BIRT

BY ROBERT ABBATICCHIO

Published by Starry Night Publishing.Com

Rochester, New York

Copyright 2016 Robert Abbaticchio

Robert Abbaticchio

Contents

Robert Abbaticchio

DEDICATION

This book is dedicated to the 78 million people in the world that have contracted the AIDS virus and especially to the 2 million people per year that don't even know they are going to contract the disease. The intent of this book is to cause research so that we do not reach that statistic of 100 million deaths.

Robert Abbaticchio

CHAPTER 1 - THE END

What the hell is this? … The beginning chapter entitled *THE END*?

Well …my dear family and dear friends, because of a random **encounter** I had in **1957**. I have been afraid to publish this part of my memoir until I got old. Well, I'm old now and I cannot die without letting somebody know about this distressful disclosure which could well have international consequences.

My two older brothers have died, one at age 84 and the other just died at 86. I'm 85 and have had a couple scares in the last few years, you never know, time to get this thing written. As my grand dad used to say, "I have one foot in the grave and the other on a banana peel."

So…let's talk about death (I don't want to, but let's get it over with). I'm not afraid of death, I just don't want to go for two reasons. I don't want my dear wife, Taffy, my family and friends to feel bad and, I can't stand to miss whatever is going to happen in this crazy world. What happens with our government? Russia and China? Will the Muslims take over the world? Are aliens out there? Will the rising sea level ruin our ocean front condo? Where is technology taking us? Will an errant comet dash our earth to bits in a split second?

One thing that makes death acceptable is that EVERYBODY on this earth is going to die, some before they should and others later than they should. You're not chosen, it is all random, and nobody, and I mean NOBODY, knows what happens… not the most powerful, not the richest, not the most intelligent, not even the most religious know. All have beliefs (def. belief: something believed in without proof) but none know. Steve Jobs, one of the richest and one of the most intelligent in the world, had time to contemplate his death and admitted he didn't know, he was afraid it might just be an ON/OFF switch. I like the aviation term "Gone West" (to the unknown).

Here's a belief I will contrive:
Scientists say that every atom in your body is billions of years old.
Scientists have made a recent discovery when doing a study on
"redlining" (the measurement of electrical brain activity at death
called an electroencephalogram). They discovered a strange activity
on the redline at death, a couple of flashes or "burps" in the redline
with the explanation unknown. My theory is that these flashes are
the spark of life leaving the body and heading somewhere at the
speed of light. Now, a more recent scientific discovery: during
conception at the instant the sperm penetrates the egg a spark
flashes. Now, doesn't that make you wonder?

Now, some humor about death: A couple of years ago I started
having "spells," not attacks, not seizures, but "spells, which made
me think something horribly wrong in my body. After blood tests,
urine tests, MRIs, EKGs, x-rays, stress tests, and even brain scans,
the doctors could not diagnose the problem. This continued, causing
me to have anxiety attacks with depression setting in. I couldn't eat,
I couldn't sleep, I paced around all day. I was driving my wife,
Taffy, crazy. I can say she saved my life, because she got so irritated
with me that she said, "If you don't get over this I'm going to kill
you!" I got better. The doctors tried everything and said the only
thing left is a psychiatrist, Taffy and friends said maybe we should
have done that first.

I like guys who write their own obituaries, they always add some
humor. There was a guy in Orlando, who wrote his own obituary,
said, "He hated hospice, and he was never going to go back."

Another one said, "in lieu of flowers, do not vote for Trump."

Doctors have discovered a new treatment called bacteriotherapathy
(fecal transplantation). It is the transfer of stool from a healthy donor
into the gastrointestinal tract of a person suffering from a potentially
fatal disease caused by the over growth of a bad bacteria. My friends
say I would be a good donor and make many people happy as a
donor when I die, because they say I'm always full of shit.

Here's hoping I can end this book before the end of me. That random **encounter** in **1957** has haunted me and has become a major portion of this memoir, hence the title *THE BIRTH OF DEATH*. I have been afraid to write about it until I got old...so here goes.

Robert Abbaticchio

CHAPTER 2 - THE ENCOUNTER

I wish it would have never happened.

It's like self-hypnosis. My mind goes back...it's 1957.

Commissioned as an officer in the Air force upon graduation from college, I was assigned to flight training. Near the end of the final phase of training we received instruction in a course entitled "Special Weapons." The course was classified as "Secret."

We all liked the course - no books, you can't take notes, and there are no tests. Here we learn about the latest weapons in our military arsenal, and their tactical and strategic uses. Tactical weapons are used in the field to kill or incapacitate, strategic weapons are aimed at the will and ability of the enemy to wage war. We learned about all the different kinds of bombs, including the atomic bomb, and chemical weapons- anthrax, mustard, nerve gas, bacteriological, including a fungus that could wipe out all the cattle in a country within six months, and some kind of fungus that was designed to spread into the population. All kinds of missiles - guided and unguided.

The nuclear weapon, of course, riveted our attention. It might be the one weapon we would have to deal with. The part that intrigued us the most was what Julius and Ethel Rosenberg were executed for, and which now is common knowledge. At the time of the development of the atomic bomb the nuclear scientists had the problem of getting an explosion to cause the uranium to get to critical mass to start the chain reaction. They designed dynamite into such a shape that instead of exploding it would implode (explode inward) at exactly the same force at the same instant to the uranium in the center of a ball. Turns out that the shape of these dynamite panels were the same as the panels on a soccer ball. The Rosenbergs made a hand drawn sketch of the workings of this design and sold it to the Russians.

The instructor was a civilian and not on the base staff. He was brought in for this class only. I cannot give the instructor's name or identify the Air Force base where I took this training. The FBI could find this information within a half day's work. The reason is, if the FBI goes to the trouble of identifying the instructor and the base, I will know that somebody in the Pentagon knows what I am about to disclose is the truth and is imminent trouble. If it were some imaginary conspiracy tale they wouldn't even bother to investigate. Actually, I cannot recall the instructor's name, I was always bad with names. It's peculiar with pilots, they remember every flight instructor they ever flew with, but not remember one classroom instructor. I will refer to the instructor as Mr. Swift (Special Weapons Instructor for Training.)

Here's where the random chance of ever meeting Mr. Swift again defies all odds. After the week's grueling jet training about five of us students decide to go to the officer's club for happy hour. We never went to the club, we always headed for the big city on the weekend to site see, bar hop and chase the girls. One time, three of us that like classical music, went to a symphony orchestra performance. I'll never forget Boris, one of my buddies, getting tears in his eyes at the crescendo of *The Sleeping Beauty* by Tchaikovsky, then, the conductor's baton broke and flew into the air and landed in my lap. The audience gave me an applause. Today I still have the broken baton in my souvenir box in the attic.

The only reason we went to the club was that there were free drinks during happy hour. There was a "track" party at the club that night. A "track" party is a party thrown by all the officers newly promoted to Captain: the "track" refers to their new double bar insignia which resembles a railroad track. All the new Captains pool their money equivalent to their increase in pay for one month, and all drinks were free. They also had a banquet dinner but we were not invited. Our tradition all through college and the military was to stand up at the bar at happy hour, we never sat. We wedged in at the bar, ordered our free drinks, and start yakking it up.

More random: Of all the seats around the crowded bar there sat Mr. Swift, our special weapons instructor, next to us, and if there wasn't an empty seat next to him I would never have spoken. And being the extrovert I am, I decided to say Hi, and sat down, otherwise I would have said Hi, and that would have been the end of it.

Obviously, I cannot recall the exact dialogue, but I will paraphrase the context and meaning of the conversation accurately.

I said, "We really liked your class, no books, no studying, no tests, and interesting stuff." He said, "I like it too, all I have to do is talk." I said, "This is sure neat here with the free drinks." He laughed, "I wouldn't be here if I hadn't heard about the free drinks." He continued, "I'll be heading out tomorrow morning for home." I asked, "Where's that?" Swift, "Maryland." Swift asked, "Where's your next assignment?" I shrugged, "We won't know until graduation." I started talking about some of the topics in his class. I asked him about the cattle fungus, "Why wouldn't it spread and get our cattle too?" He said, "They always test and develop an antidote for everything in our arsenal." I came back with, "Who comes up with all this stuff?" He said, "The scientists are always working on what the other side might come up with and we have to stay ahead." He paused, "And it never ends."

He always referred to "they." I didn't know if "they" were the laboratory scientists, the government, or the military (Pentagon). I never asked who he worked for. We students assumed he worked for the military.

I said, "What gets me is that they usually don't develop something that just kills; it's always like the cattle fungus, or like a poison that doesn't kill an insect but effects its ability to reproduce."
He said, "They have to be on top of everything to stay ahead."

We started to act like old buddies; the drinks probably helped with the camaraderie. We talked about the scientists, how they come up with stuff, no matter how horrendous. We agreed that morality is not their problem: they do not use the weapon, that's the responsibility of the decision makers. He explained that most weapons are all about statistical models, with control groups and tests. Even the atomic bomb is reduced to statistical models of the destruction and probable deaths and casualties, and, there's an antidote developed for the radiation.

We were interrupted by my buddies next to us, talking about a plane crash that just happened near our base and it was a big secret. I joined in. After comparing notes of what we heard, we figured it was a U-2. The plane was supposed to be secret but somehow we knew all about it, from things we "heard." We knew about how high it could go; we knew how the engine fuel control system allowed it to go that high. And, we assumed it was probably flying over Russia - why else have it? I turned back to Mr. Swift, he was all ears; I don't think he even knew about the U-2, or maybe didn't want to talk about it.

I was ready to order another drink and asked Swift if he wanted one, I told him I was paying. We laughed, (the drinks are free). We got our drinks, had a sip, and were quiet for a little bit as we looked over the boisterous crowd.

He broke the silence with: "Do you know what the thymus gland is?" I said, "The only thing I know about it was from high school health class. It's a gland in infants that keeps them from getting sick and it goes away as they get older."

He explained that scientists just recently completed research on the thymus gland and discovered how our immune system works. He said, "They're working on a bug to make the immunity system work in reverse to take immunity away." I asked "What will that do?" He said," If you get a scratch and it turns into an infection, you die; if you get a cold and it turns into pneumonia, you die; if you get sick from anything, you die." I said, "Wow! That's a good one they came up with."

He stated the theory is: there are a lot more injuries and sicknesses in battle than deaths, and these injuries and sicknesses are more of a burden than deaths to logistics. With this bug they will end up dying anyway with more deaths than the actual shooting war, and as a strategic weapon you could infect the population.

Swift goes on to say, "They're having difficulty with how to administer this bug." I said, "Put it in a bomb or in their water." He said, "It doesn't work that way." He continued, "Everything in our arsenal has been tested over and over, the bombs, the chemicals, and the germ warfare stuff." He asked, "Who would YOU test?" I said, "Rats and monkeys." "Only works on humans," he quickly replies. Then I added, "I heard that prisoners often volunteer to get preferential treatment; I would think they would be good because they are in your control." He nods yes, "We have used our own troops because of that reason: they can be controlled for monitoring." I said, "Yeah, my brother is in the Army and was sent to sit in on an atomic bomb test in Nevada." We were quiet for a bit. I came up with, "I have heard of college students volunteering for medical tests to earn a few bucks." Again he nods yes.

We pause again. The guys next to us are getting loud, talking about flying, girls, and where their next assignment might be.

I blurt out to Swift, "How in the heck do you make a bug?" He took a deep breath and said, "Well…they came up with the filthiest thing in the world for this bug." I gasped, "Yikes! What could that be?" He said, "The filthiest thing they came up with was a combination of human excrement and pigs' blood." He adds, "They call it slurry…that's what they grow this bug in." I blurt, "Yuck, no wonder the Arabs don't like pigs!" I quickly add, "But where does the bug come from?"

Before he gets a word out, our guys next to us start to chant, "SQUEAT, SQUEAT, SQUEAT!!" It's a stupid expression we came up with at the previous base where we first met and started flying training. The horseplay from college days still remains. "SQUEAT" stands for "LET'S GO EAT" when said quickly. We all start leaving. I patted Swift on the shoulder and said, "Bye." He

15

smiled, gave a half wave and half salute. I never saw or heard about him again. I never heard anything more about any immunity weapon. Actually, how would I know? The project was secret.

It never crossed my mind again …until June 29, 1982.

CHAPTER 3 - RANDOMNESS

If there were to be a theme to this memoir it would be the effect of randomness in our lives. I will use the term random many times, as my entire living experience was steered by random events. All my decisions, plans, and goals were the victims of random events and my will power dictated by the random gene mutations in my make-up. Randomness is meaningless because it is exactly that, no reason, by chance, no pattern, and no prediction. Disasters are random and miracles are random, and, as it has been said, the only sure thing is uncertainty. It's not the random cards you're dealt in life but, it's how you play them.

There's a lot of...you wouldn't believe what happens!... you can't imagine what's next! ...what are the chances?

A good example is my dear wife, Taffy. During my military tour in the Air Force I had been sent to many bases and had dated many girls. On my final move there were any number of locations I could have been assigned to, and by chance, ended up in Orlando Florida. After a few years at that location and after dating a few girls there, I happened to be out one night, hitting a few bars with an Air Force buddy. We became bored and decided to move on. He suggested getting some pizza. I told him there was no pizza shop in town. He said there was a new one that just opened, so we went. If we would have arrived a few minutes earlier or 20 seconds later, delayed by a red light, I would never have met her. As we entered the pizza shop she was leaving with a girl-friend. As we passed in the door way I came up with some humorous pick up line and we laughed. We ended up talking and I got her phone number. We have been married for 56 years as I write this. With 56 years of this random stuff she admits our life has never been dull.

Robert Abbaticchio

CHAPTER 4 - THINGS I'LL NEVER FORGET - COLLEGE

This memoir is a collection of memories in my life that I will never forget, especially the memory of that **conversation** in **1957**.

My college days, at the University of Pittsburgh, were pure drudgery, no fraternity, no parties, except happy hour on Fridays at Harry's Tavern (Pitt and Carnegie Tech alumni will have fond memories of that place.) I was 2 years older than my college and Air Force friends because I worked for 2 years in a steel mill after high school so that I could buy a car and save for college. My father obtained a political scholarship which paid half my tuition, I worked my way through college for the rest of it. I will forever be grateful for those giving me the jobs so I could survive, even though I had to worked like a dog. US Steel hired us college kids in the summer, they probably could have done without us. My sophomore year I had odd jobs, one was in the library of the University of Pittsburgh at 50 cents an hour. My junior year I scheduled my classes for 3 days a week and worked at J&L Steel the other 2 days and weekends. My senior year the US Postal Service hired us college kids at the downtown Pittsburgh post office as temps for the mail rush at 5 o'clock each day. During the Christmas mail rush we worked 12 hour shifts. I am also ever grateful for the owner of a gas station along my commute to school that gave me used oil for my oil burning Studebaker and gave me credit.

Harry's tavern was a neat old neighborhood bar. Harrys was frequented by those students not affiliated with a fraternity, we were called independents. Most were like me, working our way through college. Every Friday at happy hour the place was jammed wall to wall with standing, drinking students, sometimes all singing together with the juke box. One student always brought in a dirty, ragged, homeless, street bum named Bucky, we all applauded and yelled, Bucky!! When he entered.

19

One of the events at Pitt's spring break festivities one year was a cart race. It was an intermural contest for college organizations, mainly for fraternity rivalry. The carts were anything they wanted to contrive, mostly they were just large boards with four wheels and some sort of steering. Usually the steering was just with the feet on a pivoting front axle. The students at Harrys Tavern decided to enter the contest. We had a Carnegie Tech student's father, who had a machine shop, design some wheels with super- duper wheel bearings for their cart. When the fraternities heard of this they objected because the group was not a college organization. The group of students from Harrys said it was an organization of independent Pitt students called Harry's Boys Club.

The procedure for the race was to have a "pusher" shove the cart as fast as possible to the starting line, then the cart coasted freely down a hill to the finish line. Well…not only did Harrys Boys Club's cart have good wheels, the 'pusher" was a big fast Pitt football player. Harrys Boys Club won the race.

At the end of spring break there was an awards ceremony. One of the awards was a trophy for the winner of the cart race. The affair was not formal but sort of dressy, with guys in jackets and most in suits and ties. The Boys Club decided that we all dress alike in white tee shirts and blue jeans. We graciously accepted the trophy, there were some hisses coming from the fraternity groups. We immediately left and went to Harry's Tavern to celebrate. The trophy sat above the bar for many years. If the tavern is still there, I hope the trophy still sits up there. (That was about 60 years ago.)

I had a girlfriend at Pitt, didn't know her name and we never spoke. When changing classes at Pitt there would be hundreds of students passing each other in hallways and up and down stairs. Every day for a year I would be going in one direction and she would be going the other way when we passed. We always smiled, sometimes said, "Hi," when at a distance would wave, a couple of times we almost touched. One day I was dressed in suit and tie, probably for an interview or such, when we passed she smiled, nodded her head and said, "Nice." I nodded back. She is now just a paragraph in my life.

I had a wheeler-dealer uncle who was a real estate developer and my name-sake, he was my favorite uncle and he always looked after me. One day he asked what I was taking up in college. I said I was a finance major, to be a stock broker then move up to investment banking. He offered me some money to play the stock market and we would split any profits. I agreed and immediately went to my college professors to see what they were playing with in the stock market. I'll never forget *San Toy Mining,* a 50 cent stock. I bought low, sold high a few times and made a good bit on my uncle's money. When I graduated I met with him to split the money, he said, "Forget it, it's yours." With this money I traded in the ole Studebaker and bought a brand new Chevy convertible, fender skirts, continental kit on the rear… the works! A little extravagant for a new graduate without a job.

My college financial professor got me a job as a stock broker in Cleveland, Ohio. I could not accept the job as I had an ROTC commitment to enter flying-training in the Air Force upon graduation. A war started in Korea and this random event caused me to join ROTC so that I would not be drafted while getting my college degree. My first chance to make a million lost, and a career flushed.

Robert Abbaticchio

CHAPTER 5 - THINGS I'LL NEVER FORGET – AIR FORCE

The first stop in the Air Force for flying training was San Antonio, Texas for orientation. During one lecture the instructor said "four of you in this room are going to die in your flying training. Being typical college kids we pointed a finger at each other and smirked, "you, not me." The point of the instructor was for us to get serious about training. Well…he hit it perfect, four of us killed…two flying accidents, one automobile the night before graduation, and one falling off a balcony while throwing up after a weekend party. After orientation we were awaiting orders to flight schools. The flight schools had no immediate openings so our superiors had to give us odd jobs to keep us under control. Here's two of the jobs that surely remain as things I'll never forget.

One of my new buddies was Walter Hynoski, we called him Hyno. He was an All-American football player in college. The officers that were assigned to the same flying school became the best of friends. The two of us were ordered to guard "payroll" one day. "Payroll" was payday for all the enlisted recruits on the base, about five hundred of them. They were paid outside in a large field. There were five tables set up with about one hundred recruits lined up at each table, each table had three people with paperwork and cash. Each recruit was to sign his name and received his cash.

Hyno and I each received a 45 caliber Colt handgun to strap on, and were told to remain "under cover", that meant when armed, you keep your hat on even when indoors. We previously received about one hours training in the use of the 45 automatic during orientation. Well…we strutted around the "payroll" field like we knew what we were doing. A Major arrives and confronts Hyno and asks, "Did you clear your weapon?" Hyno says, "No." With that, Hyno pulls his weapon out of the holster, clears it by pulling the slide back, holds it up in the air and pulls the trigger. "BAM!!" the gun goes off, five hundred recruits hit the dirt with dust flying and tables with money being upset. The Major wrestles the gun from Hyno. To clear your weapon, you are supposed to remove the magazine, then pull the slide back. Hyno just did it backwards. The Major ordered Hyno to go to the library and write up an essay on the operation of the Colt 45 automatic and report to the base Commander the next day. The base commander is a GENERAL!

The other order I received was to police the golf course: to meet and remind the players not to discard drink cans and food wrappings. They said there were a lot of complaints about trash on the golf course. We were told to wear our uniforms and I was given a letter from the base commander that authorized me to act for the General. There was two of us, I didn't know him. We set out and started doing the job of yakking with the players. As we were coming down an incline we noticed a player throw a beer can in the bushes. I said, "AHA, we caught one!" We approached the group and told the one to get that can back out of the bushes. He said, "Do you know who you're talking to?" I said, "No." He said, "I'm Major xxxxx, and I'll have you ass!" I pulled out the letter from the general and showed it to him, and said, "You better get that can or he will have your ass!" Being a new lowly second lieutenant I can't believe he called me SIR and hurriedly got the can.

After primary flight training we advanced into jet aircraft training. At the start of my jet training I was so gung- ho about flying that I signed a career agreement with the Air Force. They were happy to get college graduates to sign up because most served their 3- year commitment and got out. In exchange they offered expedited promotions and further training for an eventual command position. I did get a promotion before all my buddies.

Then, the big distraction...I got word that my uncle was building a shopping center for himself. When completed he was going to sell it and start a savings and loan bank in Ft. Lauderdale Florida, and I was to be a partner and the chief operating officer. My second chance to make a million! I put in a request to the Air Force to rescind my career contract so that I could get out at the end of my 3 year ROTC commitment. They refused. I started to screw up on my flying training on purpose, hoping they would kick me out, that didn't work and they ordered continued training.

The Birth of Death

One of my most memorable Air Force assignments was Waco Texas. I had some buddies that just finished training at Perrin, a nearby Air Force base, and when they heard I was sent to Waco they gave me some numbers of girls and places to go in Dallas. The first Friday off at Waco...Dallas, here I come!

I picked (at random) and called one of the numbers in my "black book." I introduced myself as a friend of the Perrin group. She is dating steady and fixes me up with Khaki, the bridal consultant at Niemen Marcus of Dallas. She was an absolute doll in looks and personality. We went to the It'll Do Club recommended by my Perrin buddies. Next night she takes me to a party at an apartment complex. What a party! The apartment complex was full of airline stewardesses! She said this goes on every weekend, then told me I could bring some buddies to party and look for dates. So...every Friday, off to Dallas, usually with four or five others, all driving separately because one never knew where he may end up. Back at the base in Waco, I was a "top dog!"

One weekend I brought five of the guys to a party, our introduction was a scream! I'm Abbey and it went like this, "this is Augie and Abbey, Higgy and Herky, Willie and Billie." You would think it was planned, but their names were, me Abbaticchio, they were Augstine, Higgins, Pitts, and Buono.

Poor Augie, one night after a party and much drinking, he was driving through downtown Dallas about two in the morning. He stopped at a red light and something was wrong with his accelerator pedal, he bends down under the dash board to fix it and then passes out. The police get a report of a car sitting at a red light in the middle of the street with the motor running wide open with nobody in it. The police get there, find the car steaming with the engine racing. They open the door and find Augie. Augie was a big burly red head. When they dragged him out of the car, he resists, and a fight ensues. I heard he got kicked out of the Air Force for conduct unbecoming of an officer. I hope that was not the case, because the Air Force usually understood, boys will be boys, under the pressure of intense flying training hard partying is common.

Khaki and I got along great, sort of strange, it was all "business," I mean companionship and not "making out." We got along so good I didn't push it. I think she was either jilted by one of the Perrin guys or still in love with one that was transferred. Every weekend the same routine: a date for dinner Friday night, a pool party at the stewardess's apartments Saturday afternoon, and a rip roaring party Saturday night!

One weekend she said, "I'm tired of parties, let's go to the park." It was some sort of city park, a nice lawn on a lake front. We spread a blanket and laid there in the dark looking at the stars, and just talked: her college days... snow skiing...a bad accident she had. A jet roared overhead, she said, "There goes one of you fly-boys." Silence for a while, then she said, "You know, it just isn't fair. You guys come in, have a good time and in six months you're gone, then there's another group for six months. Their whole life is about flying and where they're going next, then they're gone." Now I understand our sort of platonic relationship. I think she was starting to like me, but I'm just one of them, and I'll be gone in a few months. Where to? I will not know until graduation.

Being a bridal consultant at Neiman Marcus, Khaki was socially prominent and was co-chairman of the Miss America pageant to be held in Dallas. One weekend she asked me if I would be one of the judges at the pageant to be held at the Dallas Country Club. I agreed, but hedged that I might embarrass her if I screw it up. She said I will be briefed on the procedure at a meeting with the other judges before the event. That weekend, the guys at the base asked me if I'm going to Dallas. I said, "Yeah, I have to, I'm a judge at the Miss America pageant at the Dallas Country Club." Their jaws dropped...I'm a "top dog" again.

I show up early and make a great appearance in my seersucker suit, Khaki is impressed. They brief me on the judging procedures and we take our positions at a table in front of the stage with an audience of a few thousand people. They introduced the judges to the crowd which embarrassed me, I was introduced as some sort of representative of the Air Force. I got along good with the other judges and we selected a winner. I thought I did a good job. Khaki and I attended the after-pageant party and rubbed elbows with the beautiful people of Dallas then decided to leave early, as most of the people were relatives of the pageant contestants.

On the way out I bought the Sunday newspaper to read when I get back to my motel room. I jokingly asked, "Want to read the papers with me?" She said, "Sure!" I go, "Uh-Oh" to myself, maybe she's getting serious. We went to my motel room, climbed in the bed, propped ourselves up and we started going through the papers. She snuggled up to me as I was reading, then I snuggled back, soon I got the urge. We started some pretty heavy lovemaking then, newspapers were flung off the bed and clothes ripped off. With clothes off and breathing heavy she suddenly turns limp and starts to giggle. I yell, "WHAT?" She said, "This is not working!" There could be nothing more devastating to a guy's ego than laughter during sex. Two things can happen: you wilt with shock or you prove your manhood with "date rape." I wilted. I practically yelled again, "WHAT?" She prodded me in the ribs, "You're like a brother to me!" I didn't know what to do, I usually resort to humor when in trouble, so I punched her in the ribs and said, "Well Sis, we better get some clothes on." We both scurry around, embarrassed, getting dressed. We left the motel. As I was driving her back to her car at the country club, not a word was spoken. I thought she's still in love with somebody or doesn't want to get involved because I'll be leaving soon. And, crazy me, I think maybe, as in the movies, she wants me to blurt out, "I love you!" and we live happily ever after. Still not a word spoken. We arrived at the country club, I asked, "Are you alright?" She said, "I'm OK." We hugged a little and she got out …I never saw her again.

I'm 85 years old now and she would be in her early 80s, I sure hope she found her love and lived happily ever after.

With no more Dallas trips, I started hanging around Waco on the weekends. I don't know how we met, but I met Barbara Saks of the Saks Fifth Avenue family. She was short, about five feet two, with breasts as big as a little girl should have, wild looking jet black shiny hair, very tanned, as she played golf a lot. Some girls are beautiful, some gorgeous, some cute or pretty, maybe attractive. She was what

I would call, "striking," the instant we entered a room or restaurant you could feel a hush and everything come to a stop with dead silence for just a second, then the conversations and noise continued, as if a movie star just entered.

I really liked her parents, they were the best. I recall being in their house. In the entry foyer there was a bridge over to the living room, under the bridge was a stream running through their house! I wondered what they would do in the event of a flood.

One day, preparing for a Saturday date, Barbara called and told me to dress up, as we are going to a special dinner at the Air Forde base Officer's Club. So...once again, out comes the seersucker suit. It was a dinner party for the birthday of the base commander! So there I was, a student officer, sitting at this table in the middle of the club, with the base commander and his wife, the mayor of Waco and his wife, Mr. and Mrs. Saks, Barbara Saks, and ME!! After dinner and a few drinks we loosened up and started telling jokes. I told a few good ones and one sort of raunchy one, and had them rolling. Some of my flying buddies at the bar could not believe their eyes. What the heck was I doing there? After that, I could feel the special treatment I received from my buddies and even the instructors. I didn't expect it and didn't need it, but that's what happens when you're a "TOP DOG!"

On a date one night, after a few drinks, Barbara said, out of the clear blue, "Let's get married!" There had never been any talk about love or even going steady. Even though she was gorgeous, intelligent, and apparently wealthy (she once said she was to get a few million when she turned 21). That scared me because I thought she just wanted to do something crazy and exciting. I acted like she was joking, I said, "Do you realize what a big deal that would be?" She said, "No, let's just run away and get married!" I go, "Ya, Ya, Ya," and laughed it off. We had a few more party type dates and drifted apart.

About three years after leaving Waco, I'm out of the Air Force living in my small home town with wife and child. I get a phone call at 2 in the morning. It's Jan, a girl I had dated in Waco. My heart pounds, the first thing I think is that she has a three year- old child and needs help. I hear load music in the background, she said, "We're having a party and your name came up. We decided to call, wish you were here." I almost cried. I must have been some wild and crazy guy. About a week before graduation from Waco, we are given a list of bases that had openings for us. We were to make three choices in order of preference. They will assign us according to class standing and our preference. I chose Pine Castle Air Force Base in Orlando, Florida as my first preference. Florida would be nice and I have some relatives in south Florida. I ended up in Orlando Florida and as random fate would have it that's where I met and married my wife, Taffy.

I learned how to become one of the "top dogs" in the Air Force: be one of the last ones to leave a party. The top dogs in the squadron including the squadron commander are always last to leave the party. After a night of drinking and camaraderie the talk is a lot less guarded and if you are there, you are included. After a couple parties you are part of the group which can result in preferential treatment during day to day operations. I must qualify this strategy…you can't be some bozo dickhead and think you can get ahead by hanging around after the party. You have to be the type that likes to stay late, have the personality, and be sharp enough to be accepted.

One day while on duty my commanding officer received a telegram meant for me. Talk about random…My favorite uncle was killed in an automobile accident on the way home from the grand opening of his shopping center. Knowing him, there was some drinking going on and he also always drove fast, the accident happened at 2 in the morning, the Cadillac convertible went straight on a curve in the highway. He had prepared to move to Florida the next day. There went my second chance to make a million.

All of us in the squadron were close knit buddies, we flew together, and we partied together. We were even buddies with our squadron commander who had his office on the flight line, we could poke our head in without knocking at any time. One day I received notice to report to him in his formal office on base. Nobody ever goes to that office, I worried that I had done something wrong. I report to him in the formal saluting manner, and he yells, "Abbey, what in the hell are you trying to do to me?" He hands me a paper, it was a notice from a United States congressman asking my commander what he was doing to get me discharged from the Air Force, and ordered him to report weekly. I quickly told him I knew nothing about it. That night I called home to see where that came from. It was from an aunt of mine that was running the family business and wanted me out to take over the business. I explained and apologized to my squadron commander, we remained buddies, but, I received a discharge within a month.

CHAPTER 6 - BACK TO THE FUTURE

All of a sudden...a new life! Taffy and I, a baby and dog, head for Pennsylvania. The business was real estate, insurance, and a savings and loan bank branch office.

After all the college education and 3 years training in the Air Force, it's back to school to get my real estate broker's and insurance broker's licenses.

Those were good years. My family had settled in this little town of Ellwood City, Pennsylvania in the late 1890s, so we were sort of socially prominent. We not only knew our neighbors, but we also knew their parents, where they lived, and their reputations. Taffy and I were good friends with about 20 twenty couples, when we had a party the others always reciprocated, so, there were many parties and golf outings. At Christmas time you can imagine how hectic, with each couple planning a party, it was two and three parties a week. We did our civic duties, Taffy was president of the Junior Women's Club and I, president of the Jaycees.

I ran for a political office once, and lost. That's another series of random events. Since I was sort of prominent, had a good reputation, and was well known, the Democratic Party asked if I would run for the county Treasurer position. My first thought was, it might be good for business, so I agreed. Taffy organized a group of very pretty girls, wearing straw hats with my name on, and we hit the campaign trail. I spent a lot of money, let my business drift, went to many spaghetti dinners, and made a lot of off-hand speeches. It was a grind, but near the end, things looked good and it became a game.

About one week to go and you would not believe what happens... One of my "spies" said he heard that our U.S. congressman, a Democrat, was supporting my opponent, a Republican! I was mad as hell. I decided to go see him. Can you believe, back then, you could look up your congressman's home address, go knock at his door at night, and HE answers the door? As mad as I was I could have been some kind of nut and shot him. Well… he invites me in, sits me down, and explains the situation. He said, in politics sometimes there are things you have to do. He said I was new in politics and I will learn. He said I was doing a good job and he really appreciated my good effort. He shakes my hand and said, "Next time I'll see to it that you win. Well…I leave his house feeling like a hero. Leave it to a politician to double cross you and then make you feel like he did it for you…I didn't lose by much.

My father worked for US Steel which was a large manufacturing plant and the major employer in our home town. One day he sat me down and said, "I have something to tell you and you cannot tell anybody, the steel mill is going to close in two years." We had an uncle that was pretty high up in US Steel headquarters in Pittsburgh, he tipped my father about the closing and warned him not to tell anybody. My father said if we wanted to sell out and leave town, that's our decision. The only advice he gave was, "Don't spend the rest of your life regretting what you should have done and didn't." Then he added, "Like me."

Taffy and I decided the sell our house and business and move back to Florida, but, how can we do this without telling anybody. You can't imagine how it happens. I was a member of a savings and loan association organization, which had an annual golf outing and banquet. The conference that year was at an exclusive country club with golf, drinks, and a banquet with prizes awarded, all paid for by the organization. The golf foursomes were teamed by random. I did not know any of my golf partners. One of them was in the same business with the same bank as I was, but in another city. During the golf play I asked him if he might be interested in expanding with another branch office. He was interested in the idea of having another branch office and would give me a call. We made arrangements for him to inspect my building and business. We agreed on price and he bought it, with an agreement that he would not tell anybody. The reason I gave him was that a lot of people owed me money and if they knew of the sale they may not pay up. I could not refer to the steel mill closing.

Now, how can we sell the house without advertising or telling anybody why we are leaving town? We lived in a sort of exclusive neighborhood, all doctors, lawyers, and business people. Well...one afternoon Taffy was out on the front lawn and notices a friend, a local bank manager, on his bicycle. She thought that was odd because we lived up on a hill with a very steep road up to the neighborhood, very difficult on a bicycle. She asked, "What are you doing up here?" He said, "I've always wanted to live up here." We told him the house was not for sale but we would make a deal with him if the agreement was kept secret.
He bought our house.

Soon, we had to break the news that we were moving to Florida. Our friends had a nice big going away party for us at one of the homes on the hill. We said the reason for leaving was a business opportunity in Florida and Taffy wanted to go back. I wished I could tell them about the mill closing, because they all will be affected.

All of a sudden...Taffy and I, 3 kids and a dog, are on our way to Florida, without a job.

The steel mill did shut its doors in two years.

CHAPTER 7 - WHAT'S NEXT

It's 1969, back in Florida.

After purchasing a house in Orlando and getting settled I had to return to Pennsylvania to conclude business dealings and pick up a rifle I forgot about that was left with a gun smith for repairs. How things have changed!

The airline allowed me to take my gun case with rifle and ammunition to my seat (this was October 1969). When I arrived my wife and friends meeting me at the airport joked about this Italian hit man coming to Florida to do a job.

My life by chance continues…I immediately started to scurry around seeking employment. I found what the term "good people" meant. Referred as "good people" was like a code that insured you were dealing with people of unquestionable reputation, and, if I were introduced as being "from good people" you dare not let them down with some self-serving error in judgment or you will be out of the "good people's" circle, never to be referred again. I called on an old friend of my family, he referred me to a real estate development company owned by a wealthy family that built apartment complexes for their own investment and for other investors. He said they were "good people," and told me to do whatever they tell you to do. He really put me on the spot, referring me to them as from "good people," I had to be impeccably reliable.

They hired me as a site selection specialist. I was to research prospective building sites for their projects. I was awed at the responsibility they gave me within the first few weeks. I was to visit a site, walk over it, take pictures, do a feasibility study and a market survey for the proposed project, then present my findings to the board for their approval or rejection. We are talking a few million for the site and then more millions on the buildings; and they want *MY* opinion? What a confidence builder! After a couple months they allowed me to theme a project, name it, and work with the architect on proposed designs. I felt that if I worked hard and smart, I could end up running the company. As chance would have it, the economy turned down and tight money caused the company to cut back, I was laid off.

What next?

We had the best neighborhood parties, a covered dish affair once a month at a different neighbor's house. The best food, as each was trying to show off their special dish. During the conversation at one party the subject of my unemployment came up, a neighbor knew a guy that was starting up a kitchen cabinet company by himself and might need help. I stopped by to check it out, quite an operation: he had automated assembly lines to assemble the cabinets. He was looking for factory workers at this point and I was not desperate enough to settle for a factory worker type job.

I had the confidence that I was a business executive type, maybe because of college, and would not settle for less. When I was a kid I overheard my family and relatives discussing our ancestry. I'll never forget overhearing that our family's motto back in the 1700s in Italy was, "YOU ARE WHAT YOU ARE." I always believed my genes dictated my character and behavior. I also believed your up-bringing and environment are actually forms of "brain washing" which affects your genes. OOPS! I'm getting off the subject, this is material for another book I plan: *THE CIVILIANS*.

The kitchen cabinet guy referred me to a Mr. Nobel, who was trying to start up some kind of ingenious building system to build houses better and cheaper. In fact, the reason he knew him was that Nobel was projecting orders of hundreds of cabinets.

I found the vacant factory where Mr. Nobel had an office. He was by himself in this bare room sitting on a folding lawn chair with an architectural drawing board as a desk. Around him on the floor were several stacks of files, some being used, open and scattered. I gave him my resume and we talked about who we were, our goals and dreams. We were both interested and agreed to get together again. After a couple of meetings, I felt he was onto something revolutionary in housing, he was obsessed, and had the drive to make it big time. So…I thought I should take advantage of this guy to get ahead. He felt I had the business knowledge and ability, was well rounded, could do anything, and showed up at the exact right time I was needed. And…he decided to take advantage of me to get ahead.

Nobel was a wiry little guy with a reddish-blonde fiery head of hair, and a temper to match. He had a German mind that we later described as a block of concrete; you could never change it. He never lost his temper, he just turned bright red with veins popping out on his neck. He was very intense in everything he did or said. I'll never forget those steely blue eyes that penetrated right into your brain. You had the feeling he knew what you were thinking. You could never lie to him.

He hired me, the first month was without pay because he had no money until the stock offering of the new company was sold. However, he did pay for my lunch. We had lunch every day in a bowling alley lunch room. The lunches were all business. We worked seven days a week for a month preparing the stock offering and a slide show about how we were going to make millions. We rented a hotel ballroom and presented the show to a bunch of business people and investors. Because we were so confident and enthusiastic, the investors got into a buying frenzy: we took in over three hundred thousand dollars.

Nobel was the classic entrepreneur, he had a vision, developed a product, and was driven: his every thought was how to get the money, how to produce and market his idea. I thought he was a brilliant business operator, especially considering he dropped out of school in eighth grade and had no further education. He started a business at that age selling soft drinks and candy bars to construction workers at building sites.

In business he knew what he needed and what he wanted and used accountants and attorneys to tell him how to get it. That's why we hit it off when he hired me: I had a degree in business administration and knew a little about accounting, business law, marketing, finance, statistics, and so on. I set up his books, helped with drafting, worked with engineers and the State of Florida to get engineering approval, and worked with attorneys to advise what he could do and couldn't do when going public with the stock offering. Later when we started up I did the accounting, purchasing, estimating, personnel, and was the only salesman. For a joke we made a five-sided name plate for my desk, each side with one of my functions.

Nobel's two big faults were what made him successful. He was an ego nut: everything he did in business was to make himself known. He didn't want business cards because everybody was supposed to know him or want to know him. He wasted a lot of company funds on an extravagant lifestyle. The other fault was that he resented authority: he pushed the envelope on everything, and always used loop holes and his interpretations of laws, accounting principles, regulations, building codes, loan agreements, and the SEC and IRS, to get what he wanted, and he usually got away with it. He thrived on stress. Consequently, he became very paranoid because somebody was always after him. These two faults would lead to his downfall.

With my education and experience I knew enough to help Nobel get started, but once we were in operation he taught me business tactics and strategy you could never get in college. We went broke once. Nobel laid me and everybody else off. I went job hunting again. He sat alone in his office for weeks trying to come up with a way to continue operations. Sure enough, he conned some of the stockholders into buying more stock to protect their original investment. He gave me a bonus to return and we cranked back up.

It's 11 years later...1981...I'm the corporate Executive Vice President, Chief Operations Officer, Chief Financial Officer of Nobel Homes, Inc. Our product was a component building system that was the state of the art in housing technology. We were selling, manufacturing, and shipping about 200 houses per year and setting our sites on going nation-wide. I worked hard - six and a half days per week for eleven years. We were all stockholders and we were going to make millions.

What memories! A big part of my life…the honor of being friends and working with members of our Board of Directors, Admiral Joe Fowler and General William Potter, both very prominent with their distinguished service during World War 11. They became celebrities as consultants and spokesmen for Disney in the start-up of Disney World. I had the pleasure of working with Al and Connie Rockwell to build some vacation homes on their private island, Cat Cay, in the Bahamas, Yes…THE Willard Rockwell of Rockwell International.

In those memories there were some humorous events that you could never forget:

There was the Saudi Arabian affair:
During the oil boom in the 1970s the Saudi business people were going nuts buying stuff in the United States. A Saudi prince somehow got word of our unique building system and was interested. He flew his personal jet from Saudi Arabia to Orlando with an entourage of people to deal with us. He had a local American doctor friend acting as the liaison. I was surprised, because I happened to know the doctor, as he had assisted on surgery I had a few years earlier. We had arranged to meet at a hotel adjacent to the Orlando airport. There were four of us and fifteen or twenty of them. Our party consisted of Mr. Nobel, Nobel's son, our attorney, and me. The party of the prince included his attorney, the doctor, some friends, and bunch of bodyguards. Both sides had questions and corrections to the re-negotiated agreements which the attorneys hashed out. The best negotiators in the world are the Jews and the Arabs; if you are on the opposing side they are the worst. I believe this is a genetic thing and is meant as a compliment.

One of the negotiating tactics the prince used was to agree to everything, then with pen in hand, bending over the document and just before signing, he would come up with just one more detail to argue in his favor. We discussed the disagreement and Mr. Nobel agreed. But then…the prince did it two more times. Nobel got angry, got up, and told everyone, "We're walking out." We all stood up to leave. Nobel was a pretty good negotiator himself, as he knew they didn't fly half way around the world to let it end up this way. The doctor got up and apologized for the prince, explaining that the prince has his idiosyncrasies. Nobel yelled back, "Well, if the idiot doesn't make up his mind, we're leaving." A huge gasp from the crowd, the bodyguards jumped up upsetting chairs and tables. I saw some bodyguards head toward the prince with their hands on themselves where they would have a concealed weapon. I jumped up with both hands raised, yelling, "Hold it!! Hold it!!" I ran over to the doctor and told him to tell the prince that Nobel has a quirk of malapropisms, and with the doctor's explanation of the prince having idiosyncrasies, Nobel understood that it was alright to call him an idiot.

It was like one of those Mafia movies where someone insults "the boss," at a dinner, then dead silence, everybody afraid to move. To show that he is bigger than that, the "boss" starts laughing, then everybody laughs with him. Well, that's the way it happened. There was dead silence while the doctor murmured something to the prince, the doctor starts to laugh, then the prince, when the prince laughed we all started laughing, except Nobel. Still red-faced with anger, he didn't think it was funny. He meant what he said. We got him to cool it, and left it up to the attorneys to iron out the details. We all shook hands, patted each other on the back, and dispersed.

During the next several weeks the prince had arranged a letter of credit and we loaded housing components on many trailer trucks used as containers for shipment. We contracted a freight forwarder to schedule shipment. When it came time to ship, the freight forwarder informed us that there would be a delay, there was no space available on the ship because the prince had ordered the ship loaded with new Pontiac Grand Prixs to give out to his subordinates in Saudi Arabia. We eventually shipped, provided him with a construction manager, and got our money, but never received the orders for hundreds more as the prince proposed. A couple years later, a business friend traveled to Saudi Arabia and while there he went by the site of the prince's project. The building site was abandoned, a couple houses were built, and some loaded trailer trucks were still sitting there unopened.

The Birth of Death

The San Diego trip:
Nobel and I planned a trip to San Diego to meet with a nationally
known marketing guru. We wanted to see if he knew any more about
marketing pre-fab housing than we did, and we had to pay a hefty
fee to find out. We had a dinner meeting scheduled - we were
dressed ready to go with lots of spare time. So we decided to go site
seeing. I told Nobel that I heard of a cliff nearby where hang gliders
go to jump off and soar over the beach below. We found the cliff and
parked our car in front of a gigantic smooth rock which slopes down
to the cliff's edge, perfect for a hang glider to run down and leap off.
We were disappointed, since no hang gliders were flying. We hiked
out to the edge, which was really scary because there was nothing to
hold onto. We admired the view of the beach about 1500 feet below.

A wind started blowing so we backed up from the edge. The wind
suddenly got stronger, some of the other sightseers started running
toward the road yelling "SANTA ANA! SANTA ANA! RUN!" We
didn't know what the heck they were yelling about. We started back
up the slope when a blast of wind hit us, the wind blew so hard we
could not walk against it. We were both smart enough to know to
"hit the deck," we both reacted simultaneously without a word to
each other. If we would have remained standing, it would have
blown us over the cliff. The blowing wind turned into dirt and dust,
we could not see, but we knew to keep crawling up the slope. Can
you imagine two business executives from Florida in their three-
piece suits crawling on their stomachs, clawing the rock to hang on
in a hot 70-or 80- mile-an-hour dust storm on the edge of a cliff?

When we crawled to the road we got up on our hands and knees,
trying to find our car. We found the car and went back to the motel
to beat the dust out of our suits. We made our dinner engagement
with the marketing guy and had a good laugh about us learning what
a Santa Ana wind is.

The new Cadillac to Ocala:
We were on our way to a business meeting in Ocala, Florida. Nobel
was driving his new Cadillac, actually three days old (he always had
a new Cadillac). As we were speeding down the highway I had a
sharp pain in my back. I asked Nobel, "Did you ever have one of

those pinched nerve pains in your back?" He said, "Yeah, once in a while." I said, "This one won't go away." I started to fling my arms around to help flex my back muscles.

With all the commotion, Nobel glances over at me and sees smoke coming out from between me and the seat. He yells, "JESUS CHRIST YOU'RE ON FIRE!!" He pulls off the highway and comes to a screeching stop. I dive out, shedding my favorite herringbone wool sport coat. I stomped on the coat to stop the burning; then we both beat on the smoldering hole in the back of his new car seat.

A few miles back Nobel had been smoking and put the window down to flick out the butt. It must have blown back in, lodging between me and the seat. We continued on to our business meeting. I still looked presentable from the front, but the back of my sport coat looked like I took a shotgun blast at close range.

The Norman Rockwell painting:
Mr. Nobel had contracted a professional writer and artist to assist in our advertising for our marketing campaign. One day he showed up begging for a loan as he was up against hard times. I think he had a drinking problem. He said he had something for collateral. He pulls a painting out of a case and says it's an original Norman Rockwell. He said he was a friend of Rockwell and did some work for him and this was payment. Nobel believed his story, we examined the painting and signature and figured it was OK.

Nobel gave him fifteen thousand dollars. It's just a loan; he will return, pay back, and pick up the painting. Months go by, then a couple of years, Nobel assumes the painting is his and maybe got stuck. He took a trip to Stockbridge Massachusetts, the home of the Rockwell museum, to have it authenticated. They said it was genuine. He brought it back and we insured it for 25 thousand dollars, and put it in a climate controlled safe deposit box. He took it out once to hang on a wall in a model home at a grand opening party. It was a picture of a lady in a long black dress in a kitchen or laundry. The gossip was that it was Norman Rockwell's mistress, which I would think would make it very valuable.

As usual with Nobel, he loaned company funds to get the painting, but took possession as his. He lost it in his bankruptcy. I have gone through all of Rockwell's galleries and have never spotted it. I wonder where it is? I'll bet it's on some banker's living room wall or in his safe.

Taffy and I, with three kids, had a nice new home with a swimming pool, great parties with friends and the neighbors, owned a sailboat and enjoyed little league for the kids. We were doing a good job of keeping up with the Jones.

It's **JULY 1981.** Our half-day work on Saturdays were very casual. We usually came into work late and sat around brainstorming over coffee trying business ideas on each other. One Saturday, I'm was not in my usual hurry to get to work, had a leisurely tea and toast breakfast in my comfy breakfast nook overlooking the swimming pool. While going through a newspaper one story perked up my ears... "A rare cancer and pneumonia has been diagnosed in some homosexual men that have died and the cause unknown. They think there is a link to an **immune disorder.**" I always liked weird news stories, it made fun coffee break small talk. For some reason "unknown cause" and "immune disorder" sparked my interest and I didn't know why. I went off to work and there was no more thought about it.

You can't believe what's next!

Robert Abbaticchio

CHAPTER 8 - THE DOWNWARD SPIRAL

I'm fired and sued for:
FIVE MILLION, TWO HUNDRED FIFTY THOUSAND
DOLLARS!

October 1981 …Our company accountant nervously requested a meeting with me after everybody had left the office one day. He said Mr. Nobel had asked him to make some questionable book entries to cover his spending of company funds for his extravagant lifestyle causing him to "cook" the books. Since I was the Chief Financial Officer, the accountant and I both could be in big trouble with the IRS, SEC and the stockholders, so we decided to schedule a secret meeting with the Board of Directors. We knew the Board members would not put up with any hanky-panky as they were very prominent in the business world. They suggested giving Nobel a big a raise or anything he wants but leave the books alone. After the meeting the Directors and I met with Nobel to straighten him out. After everybody left after that meeting Nobel turned bright red and with those piercing eyes staring into mine, he yells, "You're fired!" He accused me of trying to take over the company. He should have known I was not trying to take over the company because when we set up the initial public stock offering I helped him rig it so the stockholders could never get enough votes to unseat him. His ego and paranoia only allowed him to think I was plotting against him, instead of helping him. In my parting shot I told him, without me, he would be bankrupt in two years. Well…he made it three years before going under. There went my third chance to make a million.

I didn't waste any time. I put together a business plan to start up my own company manufacturing an identical component building system. The business plan was *A CAPITAL VENTURE: TECHNOLOGY IN HOUSING.* It was to be distributed to find a venture capitalist to fund my project.

It's now January 1982...I was walking with a neighbor one night as a volunteer for our neighborhood watch program. My wife is frantically trying to find me (no cell phones in those days). "They called! They called! The people from Wichita called!" I had given a copy of my business proposal to a business friend to give to his boss, the owner of a chain of lumber yards. He, in turn, gave it to a business friend who was interested; none other than Willard Garvey: a billionaire who owns a lot of Kansas. His passion was putting businesses together and overseeing their success.

After intense compiling of a business plan with budgets, pro-forma, time lines, drawings and engineering, I was invited to Wichita in May for a horrendous three-day visit with an itinerary of grilling by the heads of Garvey's company divisions, interspersed with psychological and intelligence tests. The thought of the tests scared me, but I knew my business and was determined to intimidate and not be intimidated. I expected Mr. Garvey, being a billionaire, to be brash and imposing. I was all psyched up to be his equal. We met in his office, he explained what he did and wanted to know what I did. He showed me all the companies he invested in and oversaw. He laughs about the one he didn't invest in, because back then, he said "Who eats pizza?" that was Pizza Hut. He plopped down a recorder on his desk and said, "Tell me where you want to be in five years, and how you plan to get there." I was impressed and admired him because his only interest was making me and my project successful. That's his business. On my itinerary was a one on one dinner with Mr. Garvey at a fancy restaurant. I really liked him after he sheepishly asked me if he could bring his son along, because he felt awkward with small talk with somebody he didn't know.

One day he had a Vice President drive me around town, to see where I might like to live. We passed some old and restored Victorian type homes along a river. I told him my wife and I could go for one of those. We examined a vacant shopping center, owned by Garvey Industries, where the offices were to be and where we would build the prototype. Then we toured a huge vacant building along the railroad tracks which was to become the factory location. The last time it was used was to build bombers during World War II.

The Birth of Death

I really liked Garvey's business style, when I sent him a letter he would respond by dashing a handwritten note on the bottom, make a copy for his records, and send the letter back to me. On the morning of the final day, I met him his office, he jotted a hand written note on a tablet page, tore it out, folded it, scribbled a man's name on it, and handed it to me. "Take this to the bank downstairs on the first floor and ask to see the vice president on the note." In the elevator I sneaked a peek at the note. The handwritten note said to open an account in the name of World Homes in the amount of $300,000.

That afternoon there was a luncheon with Mr. Garvey and all the various company executives. I was to take the lectern to give a final presentation of my project. With no time to prepare a speech and not prepared, I had to think fast. Since I had previously met with each during my itinerary I offered to answer any questions they had about me or my project. I was taking a risk because these were all smart business executives, but I knew my business and my goal on the trip was to not be intimidated. I can now say I was a first example of *SHARK TANK*. After fielding a barrage of questions Mr. Garvey shook my hand and said, "You did good, you are a good communicator, the paperwork will follow." He bought it!!! We're moving to Wichita! I'm going to make a million!!

Taffy and I were having a house party one night when the phone rings, it's a newspaper reporter. He wants to know about my side of the lawsuit. I asked, "What lawsuit?" He answers, "You don't know?" He checks the court house records every day and noticed that Mr. Nobel was suing me for $5,250,000 for trade- secret infringement. I hadn't been served yet.

Mr. Nobel got wind of my business proposal and filed the lawsuit against me. I was not too worried because all aspects of the housing system were in the public domain and I had a witness that overheard Mr. Nobel say that he didn't have a case, he just wanted to break me financially with a long, drawn- out lawsuit.

Meanwhile…Mr. Garvey wanted me to settle the lawsuit before we start up because he would be the "deep pocket" and become embroiled in the lawsuit. I was friendly with Nobel's attorney since I worked with him all the years I was employed with Nobel. I asked him to try to get Mr. Nobel to go to court immediately because I knew I would win or ask him to drop the case so I could go to Wichita. He called back and said Nobel's answer was: "no soap." That son-of-a-bitch!! I vowed I would spit on his coffin so my DNA would go with him in his grave.

June **1982**… Headline in paper… "Disease that preys on homosexual males baffles researchers." The article goes on to say, "Condition results from a weakening of the body's immune system." Then follows with, "don't know what triggers the breakdown in the natural immune system, but theorize a virus found in most to blame."

When I read "breakdown of immune system" and "virus to blame," it was like clicking "immune system virus" in my memory bank and bits of memory pop up of that chance encounter in **1957**. I had an idea of what it might be. Aha… THE BUG GOT LOOSE!! I sort of smirked to myself as I envisioned an accident in the laboratory where some technician drops a beaker of an experiment and gets infected and then spreads the bug to others. The article says researchers are baffled, but I figured if I have an idea of what it is, surely somebody else knows and they will end the mystery of the cause.

I didn't think about it again, until… the next headline.

More bad news… Mr. Garvey gets frustrated and drops interest in my housing venture. There goes my fourth chance to make a million.

The downward spiral starts… could not get employment because of Nobel's pending lawsuit. Money running out. I work as a substitute school teacher and tried a business at a flea market.

More headlines, July **1982**... The Centers for Disease Control (CDC) reports the cause of the immunity disease is still unknown, links the new disease to blood. The term AIDS (Acquired Immune Deficiency Syndrome) used for the first time. I believe I know something about this, but, I'm too busy trying to make a living. That's their problem.

November **1982**... Headline: "AIDS cause still unknown, many more cases diagnosed." I think I could be some help from what I know but believe scientists will find cause and cure. I couldn't care less, I'm going broke.

1983 - I get a court order to make Nobel go to court to sue me, he gets served and drops the lawsuit. I filed a counter- suit against Nobel for 3 million dollars claiming his previous suit was for malicious intent.

Getting desperate, I mortgage our home to fund a franchise. The franchise turns out be a scam and I lost all my money. Now, no job, no money and a bigger mortgage payment. I finally got a job in sales for a new modular home factory and made a little money to keep surviving.

1983 -two headlines: "Still do not know how AIDS transmitted, warn blood banks about possible contamination." And, "Concern now about cases over the world." I start taking notes of what I know, and the haunting over this starts, I think I should do something, tell somebody, but I'm too agitated trying to survive.

March **1984** -The modular homes company lays me off. When they hired me I had a one on one sit- down interview with the owner. I told him I knew the business in Florida and their marketing plan would not work. He said not to worry; they had 23 plants in United States and they know what they're doing. When they laid me off I gave them two years before they go broke. They could produce alright but they couldn't sell. They stored hundreds of modular units in the field behind the factory. They had all the units wrapped in black visqueen, and with the Florida sun it caused mildew, mold and rot in the stored units. They had to be destroyed. In two years they shut down the Florida operation after losing millions.

A contractor friend referred me to a swimming pool contracting company, I designed pools for the contracted customers. Lots of work but no money. I left that pool business because I was getting into serious financial trouble.

An interesting opportunity to get even with Mr. Nobel and his company presented itself. Nobel had fired his sales manager, Sam, who I hired years ago when I was in charge. He found me at the pool company and was mad as hell, looking for advice on how to get back at Nobel. I still had friends inside Nobel Homes because I originally hired them and some kept in touch.

I knew the financial condition was shaky and I knew about year- end "unbilled receivables." Sam was a stockholder so he had the right to get a financial statement. I told him I would write the letter but he would have to sign it. The letter was addressed to the directors General Potter and Admiral Fowler, asking for a copy of the financial statements off the computer and not from Nobel. We sent copies back to Potter and Fowler and to the bank that financed the Nobel Homes operation. It didn't take more than a week, Potter and Fowler resigned, the bank called their loans and foreclosed on Nobel Homes Inc.

I did not gloat, as I knew from inside information they were going under anyway, I just hastened it, and maybe saved Potter and Fowler some embarrassment.

I was about to lose our home and could not pay all the debts I had accumulated. Everything I did got me deeper in the hole, starting with getting fired from Nobel Homes, being sued for five million, losing the deal with Garvey in Wichita, not able to get employed, mortgaging our home for a franchise, losing all the mortgaged money in the franchise scam. I started "kiting" checks between two bank accounts. The bank closed my account because of unpaid overdraft fees. I had sent out at least a hundred job application resumes, most turned down because I was overqualified for the job. So, I made up resumes to suit the job. I did get a few interviews, but never the job.

A memoir, things you will never forget, there are also people you will never forget. There's Kirk, a retired navy commander and bank vice president, had a hand shake that made you pay attention. He was Taffy's boss at the bank and we were personal friends, lots of house parties. He was one of those guys that gets up at 5 in the morning and goes to work, gets his stuff done before the bank opens. He had an uncanny ability to advise with unemotional commonsense to a problem. He was my mentor. One morning I met him at his office (way before the bank opened) to discuss my problems. He knew about the 5 million-dollar lawsuit and I brought up the franchise scam and asked him for advice about me going bankrupt. His somber answer was that he just received word that he had last stage lung cancer and had not long to live. We both sat in silence without one more word for a few minutes that seemed like an hour. Without a word we stood up, shook hands and I left. We got together at his home one night and as we were leaving he struggled to get up, shook hands and said, "Good Bye Ab." He usually said, see you later or such, but never goodbye. He died that night.

I started crying a lot. I cashed a bad check for eleven dollars, ten for gas in the car to keep job hunting, and one dollar for a meal at MacDonald's. On the way out the door there was a Mazda RX7 parked, I burst out in tears right on the sidewalk. Taffy liked the RX7 and wished she could have one. My thought was, she will never get it because of me.

One weekend at the flea market, trying to make a little money, a college friend, now a dentist, stopped by my booth. He said, "What are you doing here?" He had always known me in a business suit and tie, I looked a little disheveled and embarrassed, I quickly replied, "Oh, it's just a hobby." I cried all the way home from the flea market.

I knew I was starting to unravel. I sunk into a bad case of depression, and could no longer function. We had two kids in college but could not help them. I was helpless...I just sat all day and stared. Every night I could go to sleep because I made it through the day, but I would wake at 2 in the morning with heart pounding scared to death of the next day, the possible knock on the door ...a bill collector, a summons, a subpoena. I spiraled down to the very bottom, there was no way out.

Hopeless, I contemplated suicide, at least the insurance would save the house and get my family back on their feet. I checked the insurance for a suicide clause; it said after two years, suicide would be covered. I didn't trust that, so I thought I would have an accident, drive my car into a bridge abutment. With my luck, I thought I would screw that up; I might survive the crash and I'd be a cripple, becoming more of a burden to my family. I thought of all the methods: gun shot, hanging, monoxide, jumping off a tall building, the plastic bag. I could never go for the hanging, as for the tall building I would be afraid of changing my mind half- way down. A plastic bag was not bad because I learned in the Air Force that you don't struggle, gag, or choke; you just go to sleep. Monoxide probably the best, it would not happen in our home. But…I couldn't do this to Taffy and the kids or my parents. Why am I worried about how to commit suicide and why worry about the family? Most people that commit suicide are desperate and don't care about anything, just do it. So, I'm thinking I must not be that crazy if I cared. So, I forced myself to exist day by day and pull myself together.

Taffy realized I was beyond hope, so she had to do something. She took over and saved us by renting our nice home to a real estate developer that wanted a nice temporary home. This made the mortgage payment. She moved us into a small third floor dingy condo with cheap rent. She got a better job and saved us from bankruptcy. I remained useless, I called my self "a bump on the log."

I answered an ad for a mortgage loan officer. Because of my financial resume I got the job. Just climbing out of depression I was not too sharp. I made a little money, not enough to move back into our home, but helped me get my head screwed back on.

As before in this memoir, "could you believe what happens next?"

CHAPTER 9 - IT'S INCREDIBLE

How do you go from a despondent suicide case to the happiest day of your life?

I had learned from friends inside Nobel Homes that Mr. Nobel was looked for an investor trying to save the business before they went bankrupt. A large Savings and Loan bank in Miami was interested. But knowing Mr. Nobel the deal fell through- he wanted their money but would not give them any control. When I learned of the foreclosure I called the bank to see if they were still interested; if so, they could pick it up at the foreclosure auction.

I attended the foreclosure auction of Nobel Homes, Inc. The bank representative I had called was there, we talked a little about the inventory, machinery, employees, etc. and about me. The bank was the only bidder, won the bid, and took possession. Mr. Nobel was sitting in the corner crying. When his eyes met mine I shook my finger at him, meaning, "I told you so."

A week later, I got a call from the representative of the bank that now owns the assets of Nobel Homes. They wanted me to prepare a business plan to start up the plant and scheduled a date to meet their board of directors at their offices in Miami. I presented my plan and showed a slide show, the very same slide-show Nobel and I used to sell investors in the building system years ago. I had shipped and displayed a wall section, with steel studs, wiring, window, insulation and exterior finish to wow them. After the presentation they asked me to leave the room so they could discuss the merits of the investment. They called me back in and hired me on the spot! They named it Craftmark Homes.

Can you imagine taking over the company that fired you? The revenge of sitting behind Mr. Nobel's desk in his fancy office. I have a picture of me with my feet propped up on his desk. I did gloat for pulling this one off.

Depression is like an injury, it is not easy to get over it just because you want to, but, on a good salary and back into our nice home is a good start. Being salaried, no dream of making a million this time. Taffy got her Mazda RX7.

I'll never forget Wayne P. Boyce. He was an older guy, like me. He was as tough as they come, mentally and physically, 6 ft. 4, 230 pounds and not an ounce of fat. He owned an airplane, was an instructor pilot. He played tennis…to win…you could be his best friend or his mother, he's going to beat your ass. He was my neighbor, directly across the street.

As the rough and tough person he was, I never knew what a dear person he was until his funeral.

At first I only knew him from neighborhood parties we had in the 1970s. Near the end of a party, after the cocktails had set in, an aviator tends to find another, and we talked airplanes until everybody had gone home. After a few parties we got to know each other. He learned that I had military flying training and asked if would help him with his ground school flying classes. He conducted the ground school in his home and I agreed, as long as the only payment I received was the desserts his wife served after each session. I was a big help with weather and navigation. What he and the students really liked was my telling "war stories" and telling the students what to do and what not to do in flying while we had dessert. A few years went by without any contact, I was swamped with business projects, we waved as we passed in the neighborhood.

He had heard about my financial problems and why we had to rent our home. When we moved back in, he noticed I wasn't still my old self. One day he said he was taking a friend up for an airplane ride, did I want to go along. I agreed, we went to the airport and I hopped into the rear seat, and away we went. We landed at a small airport, stopped, and he asked me to sit in the front seat for a better view. After getting strapped in he said, "Now go take it off." I said, "No, I can't, I haven't flown in years." He yelled, "Fly this damn thing!" I flew the takeoff fairly good. Like a bicycle, you never lose the "feel." He had to control it with me on the landing. He arranged more flights with me until I was good enough to renew my license. When I got my license he handed me the keys to the plane and said, "It's yours anytime you want." Well…flying brought me back to life, I'm normal again! I flew his plane a lot, which caused me to buy my own plane.

Wayne developed pancreatic cancer. He said he was not going to spend his last days recovering from operations and was going to keep on till the end. Well…near the end he did everything to stay alive. At his funeral I learned from his wife and some friends that Wayne had an avocation of helping troubled people without their knowledge, and telling nobody. A secret that made him feel good. The bewildered recipients never knew where the money or help came from. It was like that movie *"The Magnificent Obsession."* I always wondered why he was so good to me about the plane, now I know, he did a healing thing for me for me and that made him feel good.

One day during business hours my secretary said that someone wants to see me. It was Mr. Nobel's daughter. I had her escorted in the office as I wanted a witness present in case things got out of hand. She begged me to drop my three million-dollar lawsuit; it was driving her father crazy. I reminded her that when I asked him to drop his five million-dollar lawsuit to let me take that job in Wichita, his answer was, "No soap." I had to give her the same answer, "Tell him, no soap." She left crying.

The bank had a real estate development division which purchased some land to develop a subdivision to market our Craftmark homes. After constructing five good looking model homes utilizing our component building system we publicized a grand opening to showcase our product. This novel housing system created quite a stir in the real estate and construction business; consequently, the media was eager to do a news story about the building system we were using. The local TV station requested permission to cover our grand opening.

We had quite a crowd that night. During the festivities the TV reporter and his cameraman cornered me for an interview. With the TV camera stuck in my face I discussed the advantages of the component housing system and how the finished product was no different from a conventionally built house, thus eliminating the stigma of a "pre-fab" house. After the interview we retreated to a back room to replay the "take" to check quality for broadcasting on the 11 o'clock news that night. Well…talk about rolling on the floor laughing, this was it. Do you remember the *Pink Panther* movie? Inspector Clouseau drove his boss, Chief Inspector Charles Larousse Dreyfus, crazy with his antics. Inspector Dreyfus developed a nervous twitching, eye blinking facial quirk when he talked…that was me on the TV playback. The remnants from my depression were still with me, but were wearing off. Being a little nervous in front of the TV camera brought out this quirk. I had a drooping eyebrow with blinking eyelids and a twitching cheek on one side. The TV people thought I did this on purpose to be silly. They thought it was hilarious. When I told them I was serious we got hysterical, actually rolling on the floor after viewing it again. Obviously, the piece did not make the 11 o'clock news. I still have a drooping right eye brow to remind me of those desperate days.

During **1984**… Three AIDS headlines:
1. "AIDS is not just a homosexual disease, a heterosexual epidemic is revealed in Africa."
2. "The virus that causes AIDS discovered and identified."
3. "The AIDS virus is retrovirus."

The haunting becomes serious; I start feeling responsible for something. I took more notes from my memory about the similarity of what I knew and the description of the AIDS effects. I wanted to tell somebody. I thought of sending an anonymous letter to the *NEW YORK TIMES*. But then, if nobody has come forward and it's still a mystery, I know others including the Pentagon must know. It must be a secret and I better keep my mouth shut.

December **1984**… Taffy and I have a wedding anniversary coming up, our 25th on January 2, 1985.

When working for Nobel Homes Inc. I had the pleasure and honor to work with Al and Connie Rockwell to build some houses on their island, Cat Cay in the Bahamas. Yes...THE, Willard Rockwell of Rockwell International. Cat Cay was a private island owned by Rockwell and members of a very exclusive yacht club. After we finished building some guest houses and pool villas I learned that the Rockwells have a big formal New Year's Eve party every year on the island. Wouldn't it be nice to spend our anniversary there?

It's all multimillionaires and invitation only. Maybe "AL" Rockwell would remember me, well...nobody at his company would let me get through to him. I went through my black book of names and numbers and tried to get somebody to invite us. Finally, I hit on one, Mr. Bailey, Guy Bailey of United Resources, an oil company. He knew I did work for Rockwell. We received an invitation!!

The island is absolutely gorgeous, palm trees, white sand beaches, sitting in crystal clear blue water. It's a small island, there is not one car on the island, and everybody gets a golf cart when they arrive. No roads, only paths leading to various architectural mansions, the marina and the club house. The only source of water is shipped in by freight ship. Too small for an airport, there are only two ways of getting there: by boat or Chalk Airways. Chalk Airways serves the Bahamas with amphibious planes that land in the water and taxi up on the beach ramp, that's how we got there. We rented one of the houses we built back in the Nobel Home days. It overlooked the marina. Right in front of us was a huge yacht with a helicopter on the aft deck, and a Mercedes automobile in a sling alongside the life boat. Almost every day there were new fresh flowers showing in the porthole windows. There are million dollar homes and million dollar yachts, some only used once a year.

New Year's Eve...party night!! What a sight, us guys in tuxedos and the girls in gowns arriving at the club in golf carts. The setting was magnificent, hundreds, if not a thousand bright red poinsettias with sparkling white lights in them along both sides of the long walk way up to the entrance.

Other than the ship captains, I believe Taffy and I were the only non-millionaires there. The dinner was on a patio overlooking the ocean. Each table had an orchid centerpiece, the meal was steak and lobster. I know these people have a lot of money, but how did they arrange beautiful balmy weather with an almost full moon over our heads? Then, dancing under the stars. We whooped it up, ringing in the New Year, then we all ended up at the bar. What nice people, so gracious, treating Taffy and I like one of them. With a bunch of millionaires, I expected some ego personalities or a few brash S.O.B.s in the crowd…not one.

Near the end of the festivities as we gathered around the piano bar I requested the piano player to play "As Time Goes By," the song from the movie *Casablanca* with Humphrey Bogart. It was unbelievable…here we are, my arms around my pretty Taffy on our 25th anniversary, under the stars on a tropical isle, in the company of extraordinary people. After all we had been through, thinking of suicide just a year ago was too much…I turned away and tears came to my eyes. The happiest day of my life. I wish I would have had presence of mind enough to think of toasting Taffy, like Humphrey Bogart, "here's looking at you kid." To this day, it still happens. Recently, Taffy and I were on a cruise and one night at the piano bar I requested "As Time Goes By," the tears came.

Someone in the crowd yelled, "To the Tiger Club!!" The Tiger Club was a ramshackle bar in the jungle for the workers and natives on the island. We arrived in a gang, all in our tuxedos and the ladies in their gowns, to wish the workers a Happy New Year at their party. Well…you never heard so much yelling, load music and wild dancing. They really appreciated our stopping by.

The next morning, we are all invited to Mr. Bailey's house for breakfast. It was the best…especially those with hangovers. The house was awesome, about four levels, hanging on a cliff overlooking the ocean. I guess Mr. Bailey had ulterior motives when he sponsored me for the invitation to the island, he wanted to sell his house. He asked me if I would present the house to the bank I worked for, perhaps for an employee retreat, or training center.

The following day we were at the sea plane ramp awaiting our Chalk Airways plane, when Mr. Mellon and his wife (Mr. Mellon with Mellon Bank of Pittsburgh,) asked if we would be kind enough to give them our seats, as they had important business to get back to in Pittsburgh. They offered to have us wait for the next plane as a guest on their yacht and the crew would attend to us. Are you going to tell Mr. Mellon, NO?

After we returned to the States I told my boss about Mr. Bailey's house for sale, the company hashed it out and turned it down.

This would be a good ending for a memoir, but, not this one.

Headlines -**1985** - Rock Hudson dies of AIDS.

Headlines -**1986** - Much concern about "Proliferation of AIDS among heterosexuals." The thought before was this was rare. The virus is named HIV. The haunting continues…why me?

June -**1986** -The bank that owned Craftmark Homes had a wheeler dealer manager that wanted to acquire everything to make his division and himself prominent. They decided to acquire another company and move in a different business direction. I disagreed. My experience taught me that every industrialized housing company that went under was because they concentrated on production and not marketing. With a supply of money, you can produce a lot of anything, but can you sell it. I told them their marketing plan would not work. With Nobel Homes we learned the only marketing plan that would work but they had their vision. They decided to close the plant, move and lay me off. I gave them three years, depending on how much money they want to blow before they go broke. In two years they shut it down and go out of business.

My attorney drops my law-suit for 3 million dollars against Mr. Nobel after he went personally bankrupt. There goes my fifth chance to make a million.

Tired of the corporate runaround, I went into business for myself as a general Contractor, which I did until I retired.

During the next years, AIDS had grown into **A WORLDWIDE CRISIS. THE ORIGIN UNKNOWN**. Finally, the first anti-HIV drug is introduced, I think...*AHA, it's over, I can trash all my notes.* Turns out, it is only a treatment after you get AIDS and does not stop the spread. It gets worse.

Liberace dies of AIDS, Ryan White dies of AIDS, Elizabeth Glazer dies, Arthur Ashe a victim. The cause still has the scientists baffled...what the hell is going on. They don't know? When I believe I know!

I started compiling all my notes about that RANDOM-ENCOUNTER in 1957. I'm going to put it all together and give it to someone.

CHAPTER 10 - THE DOTS

How would Mr. Swift know about a virus in 1957 that scientists were baffled with in 1982?

Could this really be the origin of the world wide AIDS scourge?

I collected the dots from that conversation in 1957:

1. CAMARADERIE

2. 1957

3. THEY

4. CATTLE FUNGUS

5. THE THYMUS GLAND

6. THE BUG

7. IMMUNITY WORK IN REVERSE

8. ADMINISTER

9. ANTIDOTE

10. SLURRY

Robert Abbaticchio

CHAPTER 11 - DOT ANALYSIS

The significance of the dots:

1. CAMARADERIE:
   One has to understand how talk like this happens. People just don't go around telling secrets. It's an interesting phenomenon called *camaraderie*. The higher the danger the closer knit the camaraderie. They say the closest camaraderie is in the foxhole during war. There's the "hanger flying" and "war stories" between pilots: we learn from the mistakes and successes of others. The dialogue is more serious when the participants are in the same "business," such as we were...involved in the military, during the Cold War with Russia. We were dedicated to our work and felt we were the best in the world at what we did. It was in this context, and by chance, that I was privy to the birth of a man-made disease.

2. 1957:
   The date coincides with research done in the early 1950s when scientists (doctors, Bruton and Robert A. Good) working on immune disorder cases discovered how the immunity system functioned in the human body.

   The date coincides with the first known case of HIV infection in 1959 and the mass outbreak in Africa in the 1970s. Later, evidence was found, of some 2,000 AID cases in Africa during the 1960s. The incubation period of the virus can be up to ten years before evident and ten more before death. Since the AIDS virus was unknown, many deaths probably occurred in the early days with the cause of death reported as infection, pneumonia or cancer, all the results of the HIV virus. (The first known case in the United States was an African-American teenager who died from HIV in St. Louis in 1969.)

3. THEY:

Mr. Swift always referred to "they" when explaining who was doing what. He was not directly involved as a scientist, researcher, or technician.

He never said what "we" did, it was always "they." He would refer to "they" when explaining the scientists, "they" when talking about the laboratory, and "they" when referring to the US military (actually the Pentagon).

4. CATTLE FUNGUS

Could this have been an experiment that went awry and the cause of what we now know as mad cow disease?

5. THE THYMUS GLAND:

In the early 1950s medical research doctors studied people with immunity disorders with infections that negated their immunity. This led to the discovery of how the thymus contributed to the immunity system. Without this knowledge one could not have contrived a method to reverse the immunity process in a human.

6. THE BUG:

In those days it was a "bug" in germ warfare. Now it is viruses in biological warfare, now bio-warfare. When Swift referred to "working on" a bug to reverse the immune system, he was really talking about a virus.

7. REVERSES THE IMMUNE SYSTEM:

Swift said "they" were working on a bug that reverses the immune system. The present definition of AIDS and HIV virus: The virus is a retrovirus, a virus that replicates in a host cell through the process of reverse transcription, which REVERSES THE USUAL PATTERN. That is exactly what Swift said "they" (the scientists) were working on. That confirms the credibility of Swift because he was referring to a process that was not known until 1983.

8.   ADMINISTER:

When Mr. Swift said they were having a problem administering the "bug" I now think that was a strange word. Being in the military I would have used the word deploy. And when I suggested putting it in a bomb or water, his answer was "it doesn't work that way." He really meant administering, which means putting it in the body by inoculation. He also hinted that they did not know who to test it on. The reason for a test in an experiment is that you do not know the result. They also didn't know how it was transmitted, and…we now know that because it had to be "administered," it would not be a viable bio-warfare weapon.

9.   ANTIDOTE:

Swift said they (the scientific labs contracted by the Pentagon) always developed an antidote for any chemical and biological weapons. They had an antidote for the cattle fungus, for anthrax, mustard gas, and even for the atomic bomb. Obviously, they had no antidote for the nuclear blast, but they have millions of doses in storage to offset the effects of the radiation. When they developed the "bug" they might have thought they had an antidote, but we now know that the AIDS virus continues to evolve and mutate, out running any anti-virus. Anybody they tested was a "goner."

10.   SLURRY:

The filthy slurry of human excrement and pigs' blood was where the immunity "bug" was born. My conversation with Mr. Swift was just getting into how you make a bug and, what does pigs' blood have to do with it, too bad I had to leave.

AIDS was so devastating to the gay community that some thought there was a conspiracy aimed at them. Well…my gay friends, the "bug" was born in human excrement; I would guess that it would thrive in the human intestinal tract if it got there. I will not describe how it might get there. At first the CDC (Central Disease Control) even named the disease GRID (Gay Related Immune Deficiency), but this notion was soon dismissed when a massive epidemic of heterosexual HIV victims emerged in Africa.

Robert Abbaticchio

CHAPTER 12 - CONNECTING THE DOTS

So what did the dots tell me?

During the early 1950s a scientific laboratory learned, from research done on immunity disorders and the thymus gland, how the human immune system works. "They" (the lab) were working on an experiment to develop a "bug" that would reverse this process of the immune system of a human being in 1957; intended to be utilized as a bacteriological warfare agent. A "bug" was grown in a petri dish of "slurry" and was in the process of being tested, the tests only worked on humans, and such tests had to be "administered." "They were having a "problem" administering the bug as a potential warfare agent.

The "connecting of the dots" did not tell me, if the experiment was ever completed, the term was, "working on a bug to reverse the immune system... and did not tell me on who or where it was tested.

My anxiety in 1982 was caused by the news about an immunity disease epidemic in the United States that baffled the scientists. They did not know the cause...I felt I knew it was caused by a bug (virus). They did not know how it was transmitted...I felt it was administered somehow. They didn't know the origin...I was sure I knew the origin; it was the result of a germ warfare experiment in 1957.

During the immune system disorder epidemic during the 1980s scientists finally found that it was caused by a virus and could be transmitted by exchange of body fluids. The method of transmission was infected blood supplies, contaminated needles, sexual intercourse with an infected partner, even a bite from an infected person.

We all remember poor Kimberly Bergallis who became famous after dying from contracting the disease from her dentist's drill. An accidental needle prick to a nurse...a bite from an infected person...exchange of blood during a fight... handling an accident victim...we have become a nation wearing rubber gloves.

The question in my mind was; how did all these infected persons get infected in the first place to transmit and infect others causing this epidemic?

When facts can conjure a conspiracy, here's one for you: In 1978 there were vaccine trials for hepatitis B given to gay men in New York ...in 1985 tests found that 66% of them were HIV positive! In the late 1950s a massive polio program gave vaccines to a million in Africa. Later studies showed millions diagnosed with AIDS showed a geographic correlation. Some argued that the vaccines were contaminated with a monkey substrate, but, it was later proven as untrue.

A conspiracy in both cases would suggest a perpetrator lacing some of the vaccines with an immunity virus for experimental test purposes.

Here's some coincidences that have the appearance of a cover-up: The bio-warfare lab in Ft. Dietrich was closed in 1969. The same bio-warfare lab in Ft. Dietrich was reopened to become the site of AIDS related research.

During the height of the anxiety of the AIDS epidemic in the United States, the government issued a public report in 1987, "Studies by Army Laboratories show that the AIDS virus would be an extremely poor biological warfare agent." Why state this publicly, unless to counter a mounting question about the origin of AIDS?

The media never reported on any theories of the virus being man-made, for reasons unknown they called it too controversial.

The Government could have arguments that they were not involved:
1. The lab may have done unauthorized testing infecting unknowns, trying to establish viability as a warfare weapon to obtain a contract with the military.

2. An unknown party may have had access to the experiment. The Russians had access to the labs at Ft. Detrick when it was a bio-warfare lab.

3. The virus may have originated from the "green monkey," after research indicates that it may be possible for the monkey virus to transfer to humans.

What are the odds of the virus emerging naturally (by ape) during the same years Mr. Swift says they are working on a "bug" to reverse the immunity system in a human?

I don't know if the ingredients of that slurry ended up to be the final birth of the virus, but I know that was the start. When this memoir is published, I feel certain the scientists will research and discover that the virus can be developed from such a solution and admit it had to be man-made because this was known by Mr. Swift in **1957.**

Robert Abbaticchio

CHAPTER 13 - THAT SON-OF-A-BITCH

It's **1995** .... Mr. Nobel dies! I didn't forget my vow to spit on his casket for firing me, suing me with a malicious lawsuit, causing me to lose the Wichita job, driving me to depression and almost suicide. I called the funeral home and asked to speak to Mr. Nobel's son. We worked together the entire time of Nobel Homes and got along, we were good friends. I always envisioned my job was to keep Mr. Nobel out of financial trouble so that his son could take over someday. I told him I wanted to pay my respects but didn't want to be there with the family in case of hard feelings. So, would he arrange with the funeral director to expect me after closing hours? He put me on hold and came back saying the director would expect me.

It's dark outside, I rang the bell as I opened the door, the lobby was very dimly lit, spooky as a funeral home usually is. Across the room a figure appeared in a hallway and waved to me, I waved back. He pointed to the one parlor that was lighted, so I proceeded in. As I approached, "YIKES!!"

It's an open casket. I didn't expect that. I don't know what the body language is when I put my hand up to my wide-open mouth, I guess it is awe and shock. If I ever wanted to spit on him now's my chance, (actually the only reason I came). The thought of the ancient Chinese custom of pissing on the vanquished crossed my mind. I could picture me standing on a chair, pissing in the coffin and getting caught by the funeral director. I would have made national headlines.

I must have stood there with hand- over- mouth for ten minutes, just staring, with my mind going back over our eleven years together. I probably knew him as well as his wife, I was with him eight to ten hours a day and a half day on Saturdays. Had lunch with him every day for eleven years. He had a martini with lunch every day and on

Fridays he would have three. I didn't have any during the week but I did join him with one drink on Fridays.

What memories, a big part of my life... I had the pleasure to work with Al and Connie Rockwell in building some homes on their island, Cat Cay, in the Bahamas ...the honor of being friends with our Directors, Admiral Fowler and General Potter.

Over the years, Mr. Nobel and I got along well. We disagreed a lot but we never argued. I think he liked me because I kept him from going too far: I was his conscience. After I left the company he remodeled his offices for $60,000 and bought a Rolls Royce, and, not long after, went bankrupt. I had a plan to provide good looking affordable housing to all the municipalities in the United States with our product, but we never got to it.

I jolted back to reality, I was still staring at Nobel in the casket. Death is so final, no more should have, or could have. I turned around and left him, lying there dead, with no spit, but with a tear in my eye... it was all over.

I arrived home, it was still raining, I pulled into the garage and just sat there in the dark, wondering how my life with Mr. Nobel put me where I am. Life goes on.

CHAPTER 14 – THE WITNESS

The detractors will say that this writing is nothing but CONJECTURE, (def.: formation of an opinion without sufficient evidence for proof). … My daughter was the first.

After going into business for myself as a general contractor, my wife and I gradually worked our way out of our financial hole. I only made a living from the contracting business, but we were able to acquire some assets by buying and selling real estate and dabbling in the stock market. This allowed us to purchase a vacation home, a condo on the beach in New Smyrna Beach, Florida. Being self-employed I had no pension, so I had to remain in business part time.

It's Memorial Day 2001. We are having our annual family get-together at the beach condo. The conversation gets around to my age, and the kids think I should retire. My daughter suggests that I should write for a hobby. I tell her, "I'm not a writer, but boy, do I have a story that's been bugging me for years!" She's the first and only one I ever told about my encounter in 1957, and this is 2001, told no one for 44 years. Her answer: "interesting, but it will never fly…no proof." Other conversations took over and we never discussed it again.

My answer to the detractors is that it is not conjecture, it is INDUCTION, (def.: the process of reaching a logical conclusion from the observation of a class of FACTS as evidence for a proposition about the whole class).

Some would say this is just hearsay. (Hearsay, def.: unverified unofficial information gained or acquired from another). The information from Mr. Swift must have been verified, because he described something scientists didn't even know existed until years later becoming an international scourge. The information must have been official as Swift was an official agent of the government. An exception to hearsay is information given in confidence. I became a confidant of Swift.

We all know Edward Snowden by now. Let's say you met him in a bar a year before he defected, and let's say he described to you some secret methods of electronic eavesdropping the government was involved in. Then a year later he defects and generates headlines around the world. Is the information he gave you just hearsay?

The internet is rife with expert opinions on the origin of AIDS. Just click on ORIGIN OF AIDS on Google and there are theories, conspiracies, research, studies, calculations, analysis, investigations, and many books written. They all conclude that AIDS either originated from the African chimp or it was man-made. None have proved their case…it's all must have, could have, possible, probable, etc.

Before writing this book I did some research… not to help prove my case, but to give the experts the information they needed to PROVE THEIR CASES.

Here are some very prominent experts and their conclusions:

Dr. ROBERT B. STRECKER, M.D., Ph.D., pathologist.
Dr. Strecker and his brother, attorney Theodore A. Strecker, were hired by the HMO for the Security Pacific Bank of California in 1983 to assess the potential impact of AIDS on the health organization. After exhaustive research they were convinced that the AIDS virus was man-made. After publishing their findings, Theodore Strecker committed suicide in 1988. According to friends and relatives the death was very suspicious. Dr. Strecker disappeared for five years while he compiled "The Strecker Memorandum" to document his findings, which is available as a DVD on his web site.

DOUGLAS HUFF Sr., Illinois State Representative.
Mr. Huff was very vocal about Dr. Strecker's research, he contacted many government officials in Washington wanting somebody to do something about it, claiming a cover-up. He was found dead in 1988 apparently from a drug overdose. His friends and relatives were very suspicious about his death. The official ruling was a stroke. (Here again for conspiracy buffs, two suspicious suicides during the initial research on the origin of AIDS.)

Dr. WILLIAM CAMPBELL DOUGLASS, M.D., alternative medicine promoter. Dr. Douglass had a reputation promoting dubious health food and alternative medicine cures. He did research on the AIDS epidemic and wrote several books on the subject. One was *"Who Murdered Africa,"* a book in 1987 about a conspiracy theory claiming the World Health Organization was behind the immunity testing in Africa. He did statistical studies claiming the virus had to be man-made. I liked his argument that the AIDS virus could not have originated with the "green monkey" theory, as AIDS appeared on three continents simultaneously: "was the green monkey a jet pilot?"

Dr. DONALD M. MacARTHUR, a high level Defense Department biological research administrator. During a senate hearing in 1970, he testified there was research going on at the Fort Detrick labs to develop a super-germ as part of our bio-warfare program. It would be a highly effective killing agent because the immune system would be powerless against it. He was testifying to secure funding to continue the program.

EDWARD HOOPER, British research journalist.
Edward Hooper traveled to Africa to do research on the AIDS epidemic there and authored the book *"The River"* in 1999. He believed that HIV could be traced to the testing of a polio vaccine called chat. This vaccine was given to about a million people in the Belgian Congo, Ruanda, and Urundi in the late 1950s. Chat was a polio vaccine using a monkey cell substrate. Hooper claimed that the monkey cells contaminated the vaccine with chimp SIV causing a large number of people in those areas contracting HIV. SIV is a simian immunodeficiency virus which has infected a host chimp which could mutate into HIV and be passed on to humans. However, after this notoriety, the stores on this vaccine were analyzed and it was found there was no trace of either HIV or chimpanzee SIV contamination. And further, in many places chat was administered without subsequent AIDS, and conversely, AIDS occurred where chat vaccination was not administered. After working tirelessly for 27 years researching the studies and theories of all the experts about the origin of AIDS he concluded,

"IT BEGAN AS A DIRECT RESULT OF A CARELESS AND UNPRINCIPLED MEDICAL EXPERIMENTATION IN AFRICA IN THE LATE 1950s."

Dr. ALAN CANTWELL, retired dermatologist, medical researcher and author.
Authored the book "*AIDS and The Doctors of Death*" in 1988 after analyzing all the research and studies, made by others, with the conclusion AIDS was a man-made disease, but the origin unknown.

WORLD AIDS CONFERENCE and SOCIETY.
At their meetings the scientists disagreed amongst themselves, trying to disprove each other's theory on the origin of AIDS. The most accepted theory is that "the transmission from ape to human occurred through cutaneous or mucous membrane exposure to infected ape blood or bodily fluid in rural Cameroon." One would expect the disease to spread from the jungles to the cities but, statistically, it was spread from the cities to the jungle. This infected person would have to have come to town and infected a prostitute. The explosive pandemic that occurred in Nairobi in the mid-1980s would require high-volume prostitution in which infected women had sex with a thousand different men each year. The other most common theory held is the "chat" polio vaccines given to millions in the late 1950s was contaminated with the monkey virus. Some scientists claim tests were made and no contamination was evident, other scientists questioned the analysis.

Then there was…Dr. BOYD GRAVES, M. D.
DR. Graves having contracted AIDS himself, decided to use the "Freedom of Information Act" and research for an answer. He discovered in some "*Pentagon Papers*" that there was "The United States Special Virus Program." He found in this site a "1971 U. S. Special Virus Research Logic Flow Chart." It contained documentation of tests done from 1962 to 1978. He sued the U. S. government claiming the chart showed that blacks and gay men were specifically selected for the tests. The dates and geographical location were consistent with the later outbreaks of the immune disorders. The government dismissed the case. He wrote a book,

The Birth of Death

State Origin: The Evidence of the Laboratory Birth of AIDS. Dr. Boyd Graves, was black, died at age 57 in 2009.

I followed newspaper headlines about AIDS for 31 years since 1982. In 2013: "SCIENTISTS TRACE ORIGIN OF AIDS VIRUS." In the article the word "probably" occurred twice. Other equivocal terms were also used throughout: "may have," "perhaps," "scientists suggest that," "probably the most reliable," "presumably someone was bitten," and at the end…would you believe the last sentence? "The research SEEMS to settle any question of HIV's origin." This is after years of testing thousands of chimps and going through their feces in areas of Africa where the virus supposedly originated, trying to find just ONE chimp to establish that the transmission of AIDS to humans is possible. Then the scientists resorted to tests involving genetic engineering on the chimps to arrive at a predetermined result as evidence to show that crossing species was THEORETICALLY POSSIBLE, and if possible, that's how AIDS must have originated. And they call that proof.

Then, finally the latest headline in October 2014: "HIV'S ORIGIN TRACED TO KINSHASA IN 1920s." This article almost convinced me that I must have dreamed my encounter with Mr. Swift. The research team retraced HIV's meteoric rise by analyzing the genetic make-up of the blood samples taken between 1959 and the late 1980s from infected people in that part of Africa. The researchers calculated the rate at which new mutations emerged and worked it backwards matching it with the events in 1920.

It seems that the research was done to somehow find a way to connect the origin of HIV to a monkey in Africa. Here again, in this article, we find this troubling language: "A new history of HIV shows ALMOST certainly," "HIGHLY LIKELY to have emerged in Kinshasa," "enable us to statistically ESTIMATE," "we can say at a HIGH DEGREE of certainty," "we think it is LIKELY," "unsafe needles MAY HAVE been used," "the researchers were able to CREATE HIV mutations back to 1920," "we THINK the virus hit a perfect storm of factors," "previous studies SUGGESTED," "the virus is MOST LIKELY," "it spread again PROBABLY via migrant workers," "the oldest known HIV sample was taken in 1959." And then at the end, "researchers said further study is needed." These were their words and not a journalist's opinion. After all this research it does not prove the origin of HIV but allows a public report stating it COULD HAVE come from a monkey in Kinshasa, Africa. I will take a quote from another that fits this situation perfectly, they "Tortured the data to ensure a specific outcome."

I am someone who knows the origin of AIDS. What nobody knows is who (pun not intended) disseminated the virus infecting and killing millions. If we find out who, we will know HOW and WHY! (Pun: WHO, the World Health Organization has been target of a conspiracy theory accusing them of massive AIDS vaccinations in Africa.)

I am not an AIDS expert. All I know is what I learned from the encounter in 1957. I am not trying to prove anything...I'm not an investigative reporter, not a research scientist, not even an activist...I am an ordinary guy that inadvertently got stuck with this information...I am actually a witness.

CHAPTER 15 - THE DECISION

June 14, 2001... I was sitting in a waiting room of a tire garage while having the tires on my car replaced. In the middle of the room was a coffee table with a mess of magazines scattered over it. On the top of the pile staring at me is a copy of *Newsweek* with a cover story about the "anniversary" of the start of the AIDS epidemic. I picked it up and leafed through to the cover story. It's been 20 years- I can't believe it. They still don't know how it started. Can they find a cure? It's a global disaster! After 20 years the whole world is still fumbling around. I got worked up into a mental frenzy. I've got to do something, tell somebody. This is it! I'm going to publish! I swiped the magazine (it's still in my files). I drove home happy with my new tires, but I started thinking of nothing but the "bug." At home I dug into my old files and started organizing my notes and set up a list of chapters for the book.

SEPTEMBER 11, 2001...9/11 occurs... I decided not to publish...I can't do this to our country at this time.

Over the next years I decided to hold off until I got older. There would be two consequences: first, nobody would believe me, or, second, the government would get involved. I don't mind nobody believing me...frankly my dear, I don't give a damn...at least I told what I know and it would be a relief to get it off my chest, my conscience is clear, I did all I can do.

I was always afraid of the government getting involved, they surely do not want to be responsible and liable for the deaths of 36 million innocent people world-wide with 40 million more having contracted the disease. If no cure found, eventually 100 million will die, compared to World War II, the deadliest military conflict in history, with 60 million deaths.

It could be considered an accident, tests done when the method of transmission was unknown, no one knew the virus was a recombinant retrovirus, having the ability to combine with the genes of any cell forming a different virus mutating and evolving rapidly making any prepared antidote ineffective.

I would hope the government would dig up Mr. Swift (pun not intended, I estimate he was 10 years older than me, which would make him about 95.) Maybe at his age he would expose the project. Remember Mr. Mark Felt, "Deep Throat," confessed about his role with Watergate before he died. Swift would probably deny it, not wanting the notoriety, or perhaps sworn to secrecy. Maybe some of the technicians on the project would come forward, but, on secret programs most don't even know what they are working on, and are just following orders.

Can you imagine the consequences? ...the outrage...the political humiliation...every country in the world wanting reparations and the cost of assisting these countries without a cure for AIDS. And, the lawsuits from the 1.3 million that have contracted AIDS and the 635,000 that have died in the US.

The government's typical reaction to handle a scandal is to investigate the background of the target, (me), find something derogatory, use it to label and humiliate, discrediting the offender. I would think they would label me a hoax. I can't imagine spending all these years from 1982 and all the notes and writings, then waiting till I am older, on a hoax. I have better things to do. Maybe the government would give me a million dollars for me to publicly acknowledge that it is a hoax. Problem is after writing this, you may see me driving a fancy dream sports car and you will say, "Aha, the government must have paid him...so it's not a hoax after all."

I always have to add humor, like this scenario: The IRS scheduled me and my wife for an audit. While at the audit the FBI breaks into our home and plants child porn on my computer, the AFT hides an illegal weapon in my closet, the DEA stuffs dope and a large amount of cash in my air conditioning duct work, the CIA uses a syringe to inject a poison into a can of Pepsi in the refrigerator, knowing I like

Pepsi and my wife doesn't. This poison gives the same symptoms as a heart attack. When done they call the local police to raid the house of this suspect, (me). We come home from the audit and are arrested in our ransacked home. I'm charged with possessing child porn, possession of an illegal weapon, and dealing in drugs. I am freaked out and ask if I can have a Pepsi from the refrigerator. They say OK. I die of a heart attack in the police car on the way to the police station to be booked. Upon the news, my friends and neighbors say, "Gee, we thought he was such a nice guy.

Surely, when a new president takes office they sit him down and inform him of any and all secrets of the government so that he wouldn't inadvertently create a national security problem. In 2013 President Obama pledged up to 5 BILLION to support an international effort aimed at combating HIV and AIDS...AND... directed 100 MILLION into a National Institutes of Health program to research a cure for HIV. Knowing what I know I suspect this is our government's secret conscience speaking.

I could not understand why the media never picked up on the reports by very prominent scientists and doctors that the AIDS virus appears to have been man-made. You have to refer to the internet to find that the reason the media ignored these opinions is that it was too controversial. I guess it was too controversial because there was only one country capable of developing such a man-made virus back then: it would be the United States.

2013...Scientists have just decoded the genome of the Plague, which will lead to a vaccine. It can be caught by inhalation and is fatal within a few days. Once we have the vaccine it will probably end up in our biological war-fare arsenal. I wonder who they will test it on.

2013...A new type of botulism, the most lethal toxin known, has been discovered. A mere *two billionths* of a gram of the protein botulinum will kill an adult. The DNA sequence behind it has been withheld from public databases for fear it could be used as a weapon. The government deemed it to be too risky until an antidote is found (Journal of Infectious Diseases, doi. org/n8b). I'll bet it is also being researched by our biological warfare scientists, and they will surely test it to know how it works.

I happened upon a TV documentary about our storage of tons of warfare chemicals: anthrax, sarin, mustard gas, nerve gas, etc. The story was about what to do with this arsenal of illegal weapons, and how to dispose of it. The news reporter asked the military commander in charge, "Why are we keeping this stuff if it's illegal in war? When would we ever use it?" The commander answers with a smirk, "Maybe... if we're losing."

Could I be exposing a military secret? Mr. Swift and I both held security clearances; I expect Swift had Top Secret clearance. To charge me, the military would have to admit it was a secret and prove they developed the AIDS virus as I had disclosed. That would be interesting. How could it be a military secret when the government reported that it was not a viable warfare weapon? We are talking about 36 million civilians dying, with no military action, not one shot fired. The only shots were in the arms of test victims (pun intended). How can the government prove a negative? How can the Pentagon prove they didn't develop the virus in their bio-warfare lab?

In 1982 scientists were baffled as to what was causing all the deaths from "an immunity disorder." I always wondered what difference it would have made if I came forward and said I "heard" from a government agent in 1957 that our germ warfare lab had developed a "bug" that reverses the immune system in humans; that surely would have gotten their attention.

But I hesitated to publish because nobody would believe me anyway and write me off as some kind of conspiracy nut, and, I was afraid of the government. Over the years I felt sort of guilty for not doing something.

What will be the opinions of this memoir about the origin of AIDS?
1. Nobody will believe?
2. A conspiracy tale?
3. A hoax?
4. Irresponsible?

The one that bothers me the most is: irresponsible, because of the possible harm to the United States. The government will probably say, "Hoax." Probably most opinions will be "don't believe." And... as I said before, "Frankly my dear, I don't give a damn." All I want is to get it over with.

After a plane crash and a couple cancer scares I started thinking about, I better get my stuff in order; I cannot die without telling somebody about this AIDS thing.

I finally made the decision to publish. With all this stuff in our biological warfare arsenal we need a history so this will not happen again. My decision was based upon, my encounter in 1957:
I decided: "WHAT GOOD IS HISTORY IF IT'S NOT THE TRUTH."

and

Ed Hooper, who worked tirelessly for 27 years researching the studies and theories of all the experts about the origin of AIDS and concluded:

"IT BEGAN AS A DIRECT RESULT OF A CARELESS AND

UNPRINCIPLED MEDICAL EXPERIMENTATION IN AFRICA IN THE LATE 1950s."

Robert Abbaticchio

CHAPTER 16 - THE CURE

Stephen Crohn is a hero. His father was a famous doctor, having discovered a disease which was named after him. Stephen's friend died of an unknown illness in 1982, found later to be a new disease, given the name AIDS. Stephen wondered why he didn't contract the disease and had tests done. In 1996 they discovered he had a genetic mutation giving him a natural immunity: he could not get AIDS. He had inherited the mutation. About 1% of the people in the world have this natural immunity. Because he had friends dying from the disease, he volunteered to be a guinea pig. They tried everything to give him the disease: it would not take. They learned a lot from these tests - mainly what keeps the HIV virus at bay. Using this information allowed the scientists a starting point to attempt to duplicate this reaction. After losing 70 of his friends, Stephen Crohn committed suicide in hopelessness at age 66.

I found this amazing: The great flu epidemic in 1918, which killed about 75 million people, was caused by the H1N1 influenza virus. This epidemic killed people mostly with *strong* immune systems. Unbelievably, it did not affect people with weaker immune systems such as children and the elderly. The virus killed through a "cytokine storm" - the overreaction to the body's immune system. Scientists also found a very small percentage of people were genetically immune to this flu virus.

Our scientists and biologists previously worked at the level of cells, then neuro-scientists and molecular biologists worked at the molecular level, and now research has progressed down to the level of the atoms.

A team of researchers at the University of Pittsburgh, led by Professor Peijun Zhang, detailed the structure of the HIV virus's capsid, the protein shell, which protects the virus's lethal genetic material. The team mapped the precise positions of four million atoms within the proteins that form the capsid's structure, leading to new ways to attack the integrity of the capsid to block virus replication inside the body.

I am confident research will eventually catch up to that fast evolution of the AIDS virus which now makes it impossible to home in on. But once down to the atomic level they may find why it evolves so fast, and maybe even reverse the process of the AIDS virus. That's how it all started, a reverse- transcriptase. As Mr. Swift said to me in 1957, "they are working on a bug that can reverse the immune system of a human being."

CHAPTER 17 - REFLECTIONS

What's a memoir without recounting a near death experience? ...How about eleven of them? And, I haven't even been in a war. One swimming, one motorcycle, one automobile, one medical, six airplanes, and one by gun, caused by me to another. I had the luck of surviving these close calls, and it is now fun to write and enjoy surviving the second time.

Age 15, 1946- swimming:
My brother and I and our close friends were the best swimmers, every day at the ole swimming hole, playing underwater tag, diving off cliffs, skinny dipping in the evening. After a rain storm the creek would turn into white water rapids. One day, being wild and crazy kids, we dared each other to try to swim across the creek in those rapids. We made it across by swimming from rock to rock. During my turn I dove into the rapids and hit my head on an underwater rock. I surfaced bleeding badly and losing consciousness. As I was swept by the rock my brother was on, I held up a limp arm and he just barely grabbed it, saving me from being lost down steam in the rapids, which would have been the end of me.

Age 21, 1952, motorcycle.
I took a friend for a motorcycle ride, on the way back it had rained and I felt the front wheel get squeamish on the sharp curves. Sure enough, on one curve the front wheel slipped and we flopped. My friend fell off and I hung on skidding into a deep mud ditch. I ended up upside down in the ditch with the motorcycle on top of me with the motor running and gasoline running out, soaking me. It took a while for my friend to flag down traffic to help get me out of the ditch. One spark and I would have been toast.

Age 26, 1957, airplane:
During jet aircraft training in the Air Force my instructor was giving me instrument flying instructions, we were practicing unusual attitude recovery. After one very unusual attitude we got caught in an inverted spin, not supposed to be recoverable in this type aircraft. My instructor and I both blacked out twice. On the last uncontrolled dive we were blacked out and when we awoke, we both pulled on the stick as hard as possible, pulling more "G" forces than the plane is calculated to withstand without coming apart. The G forces pulled the landing gear down ripping off the gear doors, the ailerons delaminated and the wing spar cracked. I was ready to eject out, waiting for the instructor's yell. He got it under control and we were able to land safely. After the accident investigation it was found that the wings had cracked and they didn't know why the plane did not shed its wings in those "G" forces. The instructor didn't even know how he managed to get out of that spin. At least I would have been blacked out when I hit the ground.

Age 27, 1958, automobile:
I was returning to my Air Force base after a weekend of partying with no sleep. I'm on highway 77 in Texas going through the King Ranch, a highway that's only two lanes with nothing on it for about a hundred miles. I'm doing about 80 miles an hour and fell asleep. I woke up with the sound of a truck air horn blaring. The trailer truck had swerved completely off his side of the highway in a cloud of dirt to avoid the head-on collision. Luckily he had room to get off the highway or me and my new 1958 Chevy convertible would have been imbedded in his grille.

Age 29, 1960, airplane:
During an Air Force practice mission, we took off, climbed up to altitude of about 35,000 feet. It was a bright sunny day with a clear blue sky as we leveled off. Suddenly it got dark, I looked up and saw nothing but sheet metal with rivets. It was the belly of a B47 bomber. We had leveled off just as the bomber was approaching above and from the rear. Each could not see the other. If either one of us was a few feet closer, I would have been in the headlines that day.

The Birth of Death

Age 36, 1968, airplane:
After discharge from the Air Force I was required to remain in the inactive Air Force reserves. The Pittsburgh active reserves invited me to join and go active with their unit, tempting me with the fun of flying on the weekends and credits toward a retirement. I refused, saying that I didn't want to be called up in case of war somewhere. The Youngstown, Ohio 910th Tactical Air Support planned a training trip in a C-119 cargo plane to Puerto Rico just before Christmas and invited any Pittsburgh Guard members to go along. One Pittsburgh guy called me to see if I wanted to go. I refused, joking that he was just enticing me with a fun trip so that I might go active and join his unit. All eight of them were killed in a crash leaving Puerto Rico on Dec. 14, 1968. I would have been number nine.

Age 43, 1974, medical:
I was rushed to the hospital with a bleeding stomach ulcer. After a few tests I was lying in bed awaiting treatment when I heard the hospital alarm sound for an emergency. When I heard the ruckus of the crew coming down the hall, I sat up to see what's going on…they came exploding into my room! They pushed me down and tried to get a transfusion in me, they couldn't. I could see panic in their eyes. They ran out and got a doctor who was able to get into one of my veins. After the recovery the doctor said if I were more than twenty minutes from a hospital I wouldn't have made it. While this was going on I had a strange humming in my ears, they say when you bleed to death, the last thing you hear is your ears ringing.

Age 61, 1992, airplane:
My wife and I planned a flying trip in my small airplane to visit relatives in Tennessee. Almost at our destination I flew into some bad weather: clouds, drizzle and fog. I only had seven miles to go so I pressed on, thinking I could hack instrument flying for a few minutes. I had my wife hold up the flying chart, so that I wouldn't have to look away from the instruments. The weather got worse, and something panicked me, when I could see the ground it was getting closer but my altitude was constant. I decided to turn around and land at a small private airport we had passed earlier. We landed safely and met two of the nicest guys who were out barbequing. They offered to take us anywhere we needed to go. We called our

relatives and they met us. The next day we returned to the airport to retrieve the plane. We took off and headed for the intended destination airport, approaching the airport from seven miles out there loomed a mountain ridge in our flight path. The night before we were 30 seconds from slamming into that ridge when I decided to turn around. You wouldn't believe, it was like the end of a movie: when the two guys were out barbequing they heard a small plane fly over-head in the fog, being pilots they knew it was bad, and they said a little prayer for us. This was published as an aviation magazine story, I entitled it: *30 seconds over Tennessee.*

Age 71, 2002, airplane:
I flew my brother up to Tifton Georgia where he was to purchase an airplane. After some involved inspection and haggling over price a deal was met and he bought the plane. We took off and I flew formation with him until he landed at his airport and I continued on to Orlando. It was now night as I approached Orlando from about ten miles out. I looked down to my instrument panel to change radio frequency to call Orlando for landing instructions. I looked up to see the bright beautiful blinking lights of the City of Orlando, as I turned my head to the right to scan for other traffic in the area I was blinded by big bright headlights! I froze for 2 seconds! I didn't know whether to climb or dive, in those 2 seconds it was all over, a big business jet passed under me missing me by a few feet. Apparently he didn't see me or we both might have zigzagged into each other. It's a good thing I froze, I had 2 seconds to live.

Age 76, 2007, airplane:
At my age I still enjoyed flying. One day I was "hot-dogging" my new experimental airplane for a "short field" landing. It's a type of landing we practice in case of an emergency. I was to "dump" it over some trees and land on the very front edge on the runway. Well...I had an "OOPS." I was too low, my gear snagged on the tree and jerked me into a roll, heading into the ground inverted. Not survivable! During all my flying days I always wondered what my reaction would be when "going in." A scream? My life flashing through my mind? Panic or freezing? Thinking of loved ones? Or just yelling, OH SHIT!! If someone was to ask me before, I would probably have said I would be mad as hell, cussing all the way "in,"

for getting in this predicament. Well…with no time to think, I just said to myself, "THIS IS IT!!" So matter of fact. This is it…it's all over.

My subconscious took over, and flies the airplane. That's what training is all about, without time to think you react. I was taught over and over in the military to "fly it into a crash." In the four seconds I had left, my subconscious did a good job: unbelievable, at 30 feet up, I gave it full throttle heading into the ground, full left aileron to get out of the roll, pulled the nose up a little, knowing that tearing the gear off in the crash will take up some of the shock. Still at full throttle, BLAM!! into the ground. There was an eerie silence as the dirt and smoke settled down. I sat there in stunned disbelief. HOLY CRAP, I MADE IT!!I was bleeding and bruised, climbed out for fear of fire and to see if I was alright, found later I had a broken back. I spent a miserable time in the hospital after the back operation, with three days of crying because they said I may never walk again. The extraordinary surgeon operated again, with titanium rods, pins, and screws in my spine, I recovered in good shape. No problems to this day, but I quit flying. They say an aviator dies twice, once when he gives up flying and then the real thing. I took it pretty bad.

…Then the near death of someone else caused by me,
Age 17, 1948, gun:
My older brother was a gun nut and had several weapons at home. Once in a while I would "borrow" one and go out into the woods to "plink." The most fun was shooting at bottles and cans thrown in the river and trying to hit them as they moved down steam. After "plinking" one day I plopped down on the living room couch to clean the gun. As I laid out the cleaning equipment the local transit bus stopped in front of our house to let off a neighbor. When the bus door opened I raised the gun and aimed out the window at the bus driver's head. Like a stupid kid would do, I pretended to shoot the driver, said, "BAM!" My brother taught me not to pull the trigger on an unloaded weapon because you may damage the firing pin. I was sure it was unloaded as I had the magazine removed, so I did not pull the trigger. After the bus left I continued to dismantle the gun for

cleaning. THERE WAS A BULLET IN THE CHAMBER!! A lesson I will never forget.

During this reflection I could go on forever with all the stuff I'll never forget. Here's some humorous:

Air Force days:
What was the most frightening event in your life? In my life you would expect some kind of airplane incident. Mine was the result of a practical joke. When we were in Primary flight training we were fresh out of college and still acted like college kids. I was usually the instigator of the horseplay. I advised the guys on how to scare one of our buddies. He planned to get even with me. After partying one night at the officer's club I climbed into my car, about midnight, and was driving home. All of a sudden a scream and somebody hiding in the back seat grabbed me by the neck. After the shock, we laughed. Lucky I didn't hit the gas pedal and run into something. Whenever I die, I should have lived longer, he took ten years off my life.

Construction contractor days:
I received a call one day from a realtor named Gay, she wanted me to inspect a house she was selling. She told me to stop by the office and pick up the instructions. The real estate office was owned by a gay guy and most employees were gay. I entered the office and asked the receptionist for Gay. She said they were all having a luncheon meeting, but just go ahead in. I went back to the meeting room that had about 20 people having lunch. I poked my head in the door, and the owner conducting the meeting asked, "May I help you?" I yelled, "Who's Gay in here?" Well…they all went into hysterics.

Retirement days:
Taffy and I owned a motor home, which we really enjoyed. Every winter we left Florida and met our dearest RV friends at Weslaco, Texas. One trip we are headed down highway US 10 when we approached road construction and were directed into one lane of traffic. We were doing about 70 miles per hour when I noticed in the rear view mirror, some crazy driver trying to pass us when we are in a single lane. I looked again, IT WAS OUR CAR that we were

towing!! It broke loose from the tow bar. I jammed on the brakes hoping I could get it run into the rear of our RV and stop. Well…it bounced off the back of our RV and passed us on the right side, then went up an embankment which caused the wheels to turn and then turned left and went right out in the middle of US 10 with 70 miles an hour traffic heading toward it. I had stopped and jumped out, ran out on US 10 to flag down traffic. Taffy is screaming because I could be run over. One car flew passed me, I don't know how he missed me or how he missed the car. Next was a huge trailer truck bearing down on me, I'll never forget looking into the eyes of the eighteen wheeler driver as he nodded his head and screeched all eighteen wheels and got stopped before he hit our car.

Not an ordinary life: all the ups and downs in my business career, these "near deaths," and that accidental meeting about the origin of AIDS in 1957 …none of it planned…that's why I decided on a memoir.

Robert Abbaticchio

CHAPTER 18 - THE WORST SELLER LIST

Not a best seller...This memoir was not written to make money. It was written for the 100 friends and relatives of mine and... for one scientist. Most of the friends and relatives will probably expect the book as a gift.

The one scientist that buys will unlock the mystery of the origin of AIDS. AIDS research experts, Dr. Alan Cantwell and Mr. Edward Hooper are entitled to free copies.

However, I could make some money if everybody in the US, that has AIDS, would buy *THE BIRTH OF DEATH*...there are 1.2 million of them.

In the United States:
    1.2 million have Aids.
    180,000 have AIDS and don't know it.
    50,000 more will contract AIDS this year.
    13,700 have died of AIDS this year.
    659,000 have died of AIDS since 1980s.

I could really make money if everybody in the world living with AIDS bought my book...there are 36.9 million of them.

This is serious business, in the world, there are 36.9 million living with AIDS and 34 million have died...we are approaching 100 million deaths.

Robert Abbaticchio

CHAPTER 19 - THE CONCLUSION

Yikes!! It's uncanny, I might be **THE ONLY ONE IN THE WORLD** that knows the ingredients in that petri dish that started AIDS in 1957! The formula is probably in a document in a top secret file somewhere.

I will repeat the reasons for my disclosure of this "bug" in my memoir:

WHAT GOOD IS HISTORY IF IT'S NOT THE TRUTH

and

Ed Hooper's conclusion after 27 years of research:

"IT BEGAN AS A DIRECT RESULT OF A CARELESS AND UNPRINCIPALED MEDICAL EXPERIMENTATION IN AFRICA IN THE LATE 1950s."

This is not a theory of mine, not even my opinion…it's just the way it is.

Robert Abbaticchio

AUTHOR BIO

ROBERT C. ABBATICCHIO is a first time author, born in 1931, in Ellwood City, Pennsylvania. A depression baby, born in a house.

University of Pittsburgh – Bachelor of Business Administration, major in finance.

As a result of random job opportunities, he became an expert in the manufactured housing industry and licensed general contractor.

He is currently residing in the quaint New Smyrna Beach, Florida.

An avid aviator, he is currently writing his second book for aviation enthusiasts: *The Aviation Mystique -- A Memoir: Why We Fly.*

Robert Abbaticchio

<u>Starry Night Publishing</u>

Everyone has a story...

Don't spend your life trying to get published! Don't tolerate rejection! Don't do all the work and allow the publishing companies reap the rewards!

Millions of independent authors like you, are making money, publishing their stories now. Our technological know-how will take the headaches out of getting published. Let "Starry Night Publishing.Com" take care of the hard parts, so you can focus on writing. You simply send us your Word Document and we do the rest. It really is that simple!

The big companies want to publish only "celebrity authors," not the average book-writer. It's almost impossible for first-time authors to get published today. This has led many authors to go the self-publishing route. Until recently, this was considered "vanity-publishing." You spent large sums of your money, to get twenty copies of your book, to give to relatives at Christmas, just so you could see your name on the cover. Now, however, the self-publishing industry allows authors to get published in a timely fashion, retain the rights to your work, keeping up to ninety-percent of your royalties, instead of the traditional five-percent.

We've opened up the gates, allowing you inside the world of publishing. While others charge you as much as fifteen-thousand dollars for a publishing package, we charge less than five-hundred dollars to cover copyright, ISBN, and distribution costs. Do you really want to spend all your time formatting, converting, designing a cover, and then promoting your book, because no one else will?

Our editors are professionals, able to create a top-notch book that you will be proud of. Becoming a published author is supposed to be fun, not a hassle.

At Starry Night Publishing, you submit your work, we create a professional-looking cover, a table of contents, compile your text and images into the appropriate format, convert your files for eReaders, take care of copyright information, assign an ISBN, allow you to keep one-hundred-percent of your rights, distribute your story worldwide on Amazon, Barnes & Noble and many other retailers, and write you a check for your royalties. There are no other hidden fees involved! You don't pay extra for a cover, or to keep your book in print. We promise! Everything is included! You even get a free copy of your book and unlimited half-price copies.

In four short years, we've published more than fifteen-hundred books, compared to the major publishing houses which only add an average of six new titles per year. We will publish your fiction, or non-fiction books about anything, and look forward to reading your stories and sharing them with the world.

We sincerely hope that you will join the growing Starry Night Publishing family, become a published author and gain the world-wide exposure that you deserve. You deserve to succeed. Success comes to those who make opportunities happen, not those who wait for opportunities to happen. You just have to try. Thanks for joining us on our journey.

www.starrynightpublishing.com

www.facebook.com/starrynightpublishing/

Made in the USA
Middletown, DE
25 September 2022